SENECA

THE CLIMBER'S GUIDE

SENECA

THE CLIMBER'S GUIDE

2nd Edition

Tony Barnes

Earthbound Sports LLC
P.O. Box 3312
Chapel Hill, NC 27515
www.earthboundsports.com

Front Cover: The West Face of Seneca at dusk. Photo by Kevin Obrien

Back Cover: Adam Ehrlich climbing PSYCHO KILLER, 5.11b R, on the Bell Wall of the North Peak – West Face. Photo by Christopher Paik

Back Cover: Gina Hoag leading the classic YE GODS AND LITTLE FISHES 5.8, on the South End. Photo by Bill Webster

Copyright © 2006

ISBN 0-9643698-8-5

Printed in the United States of America
Second Edition, 2006

TABLE OF CONTENTS

Rich Pleiss on ECSTASY in the mid-1970s. Rich was co-author of the second climbing guide to Seneca in 1975. (Photo: Bill Webster)

ACKNOWLEDGMENTS

The second edition is based on a series of six guidebooks begun in 1975 by Bill Webster and Rich Pleiss. The number of routes and variations described has risen from 121 in 1975 to over 450 today. This book includes many new routes and important recent developments in the form of new trails and fixed anchors.

This book, like its predecessors, is a repository of historical data, much of which was written long ago, often exactly as described by first ascentionists. This edition owes its existence to Bill Webster's 15 years as editor-publisher, and to his continuing tenure as publisher.

I would especially like to thank former Gendarme climbing shop and Seneca Rocks Climbing School owner John Markwell, who lent me his collection of the earlier guidebooks for reference. To them I added my own crumbling copies of the yellow-covered 1978 edition and the 1990 edition. Included was *A Climber's Guide to Seneca Rocks, West Virginia,* edited by F. R. Robinson, copyright 1971. This guide, with beautiful topos by John Christian published by the Mountaineering Section of the Potomac Appalachian Trail Club, was the first comprehensive guidebook to Seneca. It contained 78 routes, including many of Seneca's most classics lines. Bill Webster's acknowledgments in the 1975 edition and subsequent editions cite constant reference to this fine book. Thanks to John Markwell's kind loan I too can refer to this original source. Also, John took many of the aerial photographs during a couple of hair-raising chopper flights around the peaks of Seneca.

Many other climbers have offered route information and suggestions on content and format—too many to thank you all here. You know who you are. No guidebook would be possible without climbers like you.

Good climbing, everyone!

IMPORTANT SAFETY INFORMATION
PLEASE READ THE MATERIAL ON THIS PAGE BEFORE
USING THE GUIDE!

Rock climbing, ice climbing, bouldering, and mountaineering are sports that may be extremely dangerous and may lead to severe injury or death. This book is a guide to rock climbing in one particular area within West Virginia. Before using this guide, it is extremely important that the user understand the limitations that may be found in these pages.

1. This is a guidebook to climbing routes. It is not a climbing instruction manual. Climbers should receive adequate instruction before using this guide.

2. This guide consists of information compiled from a number of different sources. Much of the information has not been personally verified by the editor. Topos, lines on photographs, and written descriptions may inadvertently contain inaccurate information.

3. The user who wishes to climb safely must have a strong working knowledge of, and experience with, current climbing methods, including methods of protecting climbing routes, rope handling, retreat from rocks and mountains, and emergency response.

4. Climbers must rely on their own personal judgment in all climbing situations. This guidebook should be used to supplement the climber's personal knowledge, skill, and judgment. Information found in the guidebook should not be used as a substitute for personal judgment, especially in situations that have the potential for injury or death.

5. Difficulty ratings and descriptions found in this guide are subjective. The ratings are used in an attempt to give climbers a general feel for the relative difficulty of climbing routes. Where possible the editor uses consensus ratings generally in use in the local climbing community. Many routes, particularly those that are not popular, may not have consensus ratings. Individuals may disagree on ratings for a variety of reasons.

6. Protection ratings and descriptions found in this guide are subjective. The ratings are used in an attempt to give climbers a general feel for the relative danger of climbing certain routes. Where possible the editor uses consensus ratings generally in use in the local climbing community. Many routes, particularly those that are not popular, may not have consensus ratings. Individuals may disagree on protection ratings for a variety of reasons.

7. All routes have the potential for injury or death regardless of whether or not they have an R or X protection rating.

8. This book refers to fixed protection such as pitons and bolts. The editor cannot guarantee that these fixed protection points are still in place (they are sometimes removed by human as well as by natural causes). Further, it is important to know that the editor cannot guarantee the integrity of any feature described in this book, including bolts, pitons, rock features, vegetation, or other features.

THE EDITOR AND PUBLISHER OF THIS GUIDE OFFER NO WARRANTY, WHETHER EXPRESSED OR IMPLIED, THAT THE INFORMATION CONTAINED HEREIN IS ACCURATE. REMEMBER, CLIMBING IS POTENTIALLY A LIFE-THREATENING SPORT.

INTRODUCTION

Welcome to Seneca Rocks, centerpiece of the Monongahela National Forest's Spruce Knob–Seneca Rocks National Recreation Area and pride of Pendleton County, West Virginia. The rocks are known and loved by many and have long been a destination for a growing number of dedicated climbers from all over the United States.

The Rocks lie along the upper Potomac River in the spectacular region known as the Potomac Highlands of the Allegheny Mountains, just a few miles from the Eastern Continental Divide. This makes for a fairly remote setting, with wonderfully intact natural values and gorgeous mountain views.

If you like climbing on sustained, vertical rock, you'll love Seneca. Routes vary from one to four pitches and tend to be strenuous regardless of length. Many climbs follow obvious lines, especially corners and vertical cracks, while others wander up blank-looking faces. Despite the steepness of the rock, many moderate routes exist, due in part to the presence of larger cracks and holds. And perhaps best of all, many of the climbs lead to the South Summit, one of the highest and most exciting 5th class summits east of the Mississippi.

Seneca Rocks are a gift to eastern climbers who are short on areas with multi-pitch routes and technical summits. The crags have provided a memorable introduction to real exposure and wider mountaineering skills since the 1930s and lent themselves perfectly to the advancement and refinement of clean free-climbing skills. Bolts placed since the 1980s went in largely on ground-up ascents—that is, sparingly. The result today is an enduring gift of adventure. Seneca has both old classic climbs that still challenge in an era of high-tech gear and newer routes to test the mettle of climbers coming of age in the twenty-first century.

SAFETY AND RESCUE

Seneca presents the climber with at least as many hazards as other eastern climbing areas and a far more complicated rescue scenario than at most cliffs.

Hazards and Safety Issues

Seneca climbers should be familiar with some of the potential hazards that may be encountered. Most hazards found at Seneca are the same as those experienced in many climbing areas throughout the world: occasionally sparse protection, poor fixed protection, route-finding problems, occasional loose holds, and rubble-covered ledges. The following safety issues and hazards warrant special attention:

1. Getting to the base of your route may require very exposed scrambling.

2. Safe leads often require racks that are large and varied, including slings of various lengths. Most climbers carry wired nuts of all sizes; camming devices such as Camalots, Friends, etc.; tricams, TCUs, or Aliens; and often larger chocks such as Hexes.

3. Safe climbing, especially on descents, can be greatly enhanced by use of proper-length ropes. The author highly recommends that climbers bring no single rope shorter than 60 meters. Double ropes are often useful for both safe descents and rope drag management.

4. Seneca can surprise the climber with its occasional loose holds and many debris-strewn ledges, which present a serious rockfall hazard to climbers below. You take your life in your own hands when you choose to stand below certain routes. Be particularly cautious when standing below or climbing on DROP ZONE, CANDY CORNER, and YE GODS: these routes are located below the extremely popular Skyline Traverse area. Areas at the base of the Southern Pillar are also subject to natural rockfall after stormy weather.

David Wormald following in the footsteps of countless others by standing on the knife-edge summit of the South Peak. (Photo: Bill Webster)

5. Some areas of the rock are subject to rare but significant natural rockfall. Two recent examples are the fall of the Gendarme in 1987 and, in 1972, the collapse of the entire upper Thais Face. The Southern Pillar and South End are capped by earth and rubble (the South Summit is solid rock), and natural rockfall can occur during and after heavy rains.

6. Winds can become fierce, especially along the South End, the Gunsight, the entire summit ridge of the South Peak, and in the major gaps. On windy days it is not uncommon to see ropes picked up by the wind and lifted high in the air. Voice communication in these conditions can be almost impossible.

7. Seneca's pigeons may seem to present a trivial level of risk, but occasionally they cause serious problems. A speeding pigeon roaring past your head when you're unroped with a couple hundred feet of exposure under your feet, or running it out to a belay niche that holds a pigeon's nest, can be frightening!

Rescue Gear and Services

If you are involved in a life-threatening emergency at Seneca it is important to initiate a careful evacuation to the road as quickly and safely as possible. Finding assistance for a rescue may be problematic. The cliff is located in a remote area with only a small resident climbing population, and as of 2006 there was no official technical climbing rescue entity based at Seneca. *Be prepared to carry out a self-rescue AT ALL TIMES.*

At this writing a rescue cache, including basic trauma equipment and a stokes litter, was located on the front porch of the Gendarme. In addition, a rescue cache was located at the base of the West Face where the main approach trail meets the trail that skirts the base of the rock. See map on page 35. PLEASE DO NOT TAMPER WITH THIS EQUIPMENT: IT MAY BE NEEDED TO SAVE SOMEONE'S LIFE! If necessary send someone down to the town to call 911 and alert local guide service personnel. Remember that if you call 911 you must stay in the town until the rescue squad arrives and is briefed!

The cliff is 30 minutes by highway from the nearest hospital. Victims of serious accidents are usually evacuated by life-flight helicopters dispatched from large medical facilities in Morgantown, West Virginia, and Charlottesville, Virginia.

Ambulance Service

Call 911 for ambulance service. If emergency evacuation is required from the vicinity of the rocks it may be possible to drive an emergency vehicle over the concrete low-water bridge at the end of Roy Gap Road. This road cannot be used if the river covers the bridge.

Cell Phones

Cell phones do not work at Seneca.

Hospitals

There are two hospitals in the area. The closest is Grant Memorial, (304) 257-1026, in Petersburg, 23 miles to the north on Rt. 55. A somewhat larger hospital, Davis Memorial, (304) 636-3300, is located in Elkins, about 40 miles west on Rt. 33.

USING THE GUIDE

First-time Seneca climbers are advised to read the chapter entitled Getting Around Seneca {pages 31-40}. This chapter gives an overview of the entire rock and approach information. It is important to learn the names of the most prominent features and the locations of the approach trails. This information is useful when using the guide and when asking help from other climbers. Climbing routes are described in left-to-right, clockwise order, starting with the Lower Slabs and followed by the leftmost routes on the West Face of the North Peak. Descriptions then move to the South Peak–West Face, the South End, Southern Pillar, South Peak–East Face on the back side, and finally, the North Peak-East Face. These natural sections of the rock receive their own chapters. Refer to illustrations at the beginning of this book as well as in each chapter. All left and right directions are given with the assumption that you are facing the rock. Not all routes are depicted on photographs or topos.

The best descents are described at the beginning of each section and/or with the individual route description.

Highly recommended routes are indicated by a ★.

MAP, TOPO AND PHOTO LEGEND

All lines and symbols on maps, topos and photos are approximations only. The user should not assume that lines on photos and topos show the exact locations of routes and features.

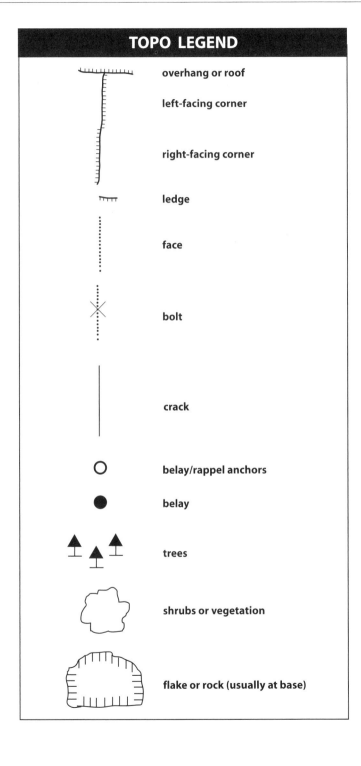

TOPO LEGEND

overhang or roof

left-facing corner

right-facing corner

ledge

face

bolt

crack

belay/rappel anchors

belay

trees

shrubs or vegetation

flake or rock (usually at base)

DIFFICULTY RATING SYSTEM

This guide uses the YDS (Yosemite Decimal System) to grade 5th class routes:

5.0–5.2	Very Easy—manageable by most beginners with a top belay
5.3–5.5	Straightforward—but beginning to be strenuous
5.6–5.8	Moderately Difficult—takes real technique and fitness
5.9–5.11	Difficult—most climbers at this level stay very fit, train, and take regular climbing trips
5.12–5.14	Extremely Difficult—for most people these grades require focus and dedication in addition to serious training

Routes 5.10 and harder are usually subdivided into quarter grades with letters *a* through *d*. For example 5.10c is a quarter grade harder than 5.10b.

PROTECTION RATING SYSTEM

This guide indicates the generally accepted consensus on the safeness of each route through the following rating system:

G—Generally good protection from start to finish.

PG—Committing runouts on adequate protection; higher injury potential in the event of a fall and less margin for error in climbing at your limit while placing gear.

R—Longer runouts or runouts with groundfall potential; protection widely spaced or dubious in quality. In the event of a fall there is significant danger of injury or death.

X—Unprotected routes or climbs with no protection over long stretches of difficult rock. A fall would most likely result in serious injury or death.

ENVIRONMENT

The public perception that the climbing community abuses the environment is the most important issue facing the sport today. Climbers must act in a responsible manner to maintain climbing privileges on public and private property and must be active in promoting the truth concerning the sport's true environmental impact.

One of the best things we can all do as climbers is join and support the Access Fund and similar organizations.

The most serious environmental problem at Seneca is that of erosion caused by climbers' short-cutting trails or using alternative trails to reach the rocks. The rock sits on top of a very steep hill that has thin, sandy soils. Every person who cuts a switchback or uses one of the "unofficial" trails in order to save a few minutes on the approach or descent contributes to a problem that conscientious climbers have been battling for decades. The U.S. Forest Service has been a supportive partner in the development of climbers' trails, all of which have been built by volunteer labor from the climbing community.

In addition to using the official trail system, the environmental impact of climbing can be reduced if everyone tries to do the following:

- Avoid disturbing plants and animals found on the approach and on the cliff.
- Plan your bowel movements for proper facilities in the valley.
- Carry out all litter, including old tape.
- Avoid using unslung trees for rappel anchors, if possible.
- Carpool to the rock.

SERVICES

The nearest towns of significant size are:

- Petersburg, about 25 minutes to the north on Rt. 28/55

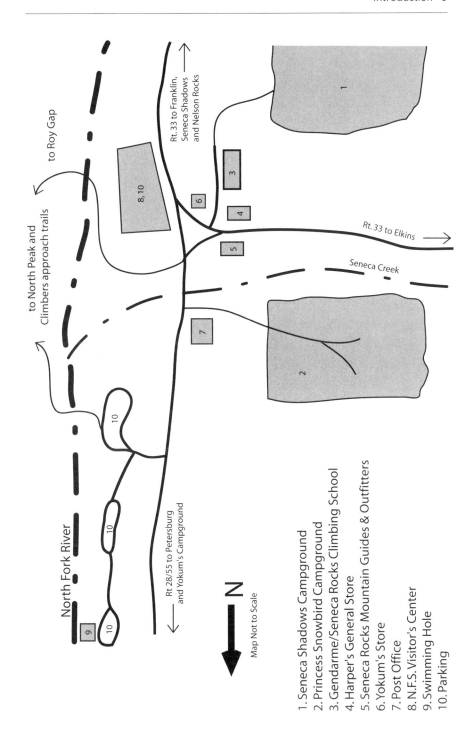

N

Map Not to Scale

North Fork River

to Roy Gap

to North Peak and
Climbers approach trails

Rt. 33 to Franklin,
Seneca Shadows
and Nelson Rocks

Rt. 33 to Elkins

Seneca Creek

Rt 28/55 to Petersburg
and Yokum's Campground

1. Seneca Shadows Campground
2. Princess Snowbird Campground
3. Gendarme/Seneca Rocks Climbing School
4. Harper's General Store
5. Seneca Rocks Mountain Guides & Outfitters
6. Yokum's Store
7. Post Office
8. N.F.S. Visitor's Center
9. Swimming Hole
10. Parking

- Elkins, approximately 45 minutes to the west on Rt. 33
- Franklin, the county seat of Pendleton County, 45 minutes south on Rt. 33
- Canaan Valley (a resort area best known for skiing) and the town of Davis, approximately 40 minutes to the northeast

All have basic services. Petersburg has the closest big grocery store, and Elkins (a college town) is your best bet for entertainment.

Camping

The great flood of 1985 destroyed the old U.S. Forest Service camping area along Roy Gap Road. In retrospect this was probably one of the few good things to come from the flood, since this squalid climbers' flop in the floodplain of both Seneca Creek and the North Fork had already outlived its welcome. A very comfortable Forest Service campground has been built on a high bench just south of town. There are two commercial campgrounds in the immediate area, and there's great primitive camping in the surrounding Monongahela National Forest, outside the Seneca Rocks portion of the Spruce Knob–Seneca Rocks National Recreation Area. Camping is not allowed on the rocks side of the North Fork River.

Seneca Shadows: This U.S. Forest Service campground is situated above the town of Seneca Rocks. The campground has a great view of the rocks and hot showers. The entrance is located off Rt. 28, 1 mile south of town. Reservations: (877) 444-6777.

Yokum's Vacationland Campground: This campground is located about a half mile north of the crossroads on Rt. 55. Showers are available. Reservations: (304) 567-2351.

Princess Snowbird Campground: This is the old pavilion camping area previously owned by the Harpers. Carl and Shirley Yokum now operate this camping area, which is located right in town along Seneca Creek. Reservations: (304) 567-2351.

Motels
There are three motels and cabins available in the immediate vicinity:

4-U motel: Two miles south of Town on Rt. 55; (304) 567-2111 or -9898.

Smoke Hole Motel and Cabins: Fifteen miles north of town on Rt. 28; (800) 828-8478.

Yokum's Motel/Cabins: Two miles north of town on Rt. 28; (304) 567-2351.

In addition, there are several motels 23 miles north of Seneca (via Route 55) in the town of Petersburg, or about the same driving time northwest in the Canaan Valley area (via Routes 33 and 32).

Groceries and Supplies
Food and other supplies can be purchased at Harper's Country Store and Yokum's Grocery, the two general stores that are located at the crossroads, or at larger stores in Petersburg, Davis, and Elkins.

Restaurants
4-U: Located about 2 miles south of the crossroads on Rt. 55. The 4-U is a traditional American diner that serves breakfast, lunch, and dinner.

Front Porch: This restaurant, which is located directly above Harper's Country Store next to the Gendarme, serves lunch and dinner. It specializes in pizza and sandwiches.

Yokum's: Located about half a mile north of the crossroads on Rt. 55. The restaurant serves traditional American diner style for breakfast, lunch, and dinner.

Valley View: Drive 5 miles south on Rt. 55. Traditional American diner style open for breakfast, lunch, and dinner.

U.S. Forest Service Discovery Center
This facility, which is particularly attractive on a rainy day, offers maps, books, informative displays, and regular film and video shows.

Drinking Water

Water can be obtained from taps at Seneca Shadows Campground, the commercial campgrounds, or the Discovery Center.

Climbing Supplies and Climbing School/Guide Services

These friendly professional outfits are also great places to hang out or meet other climbers:

The Gendarme/Seneca Rocks Climbing School: The Gendarme is one of the oldest technical climbing shops in the East and is the home of the oldest climbing school/guide service at Seneca. View the Web site at www.thegendarme.com. Telephone: (800) 548-0108 or (304) 567-2600.

Seneca Rocks Mountain Guides and Outfitters: Seneca Rocks Mountain Guides have been located across the street from Harper's Store since 1988. View the Web site at www.senecarocks.com or call (800) 451-5108 from most eastern states. Persons living in the western U.S. can call (304) 567-2115.

Swimming

The Forest Service swimming area is located about half a mile north of the Discovery Center. A trail leads to the river from the northernmost parking lot.

HISTORY

This rugged area of eastern West Virginia has been influenced by many diverse cultures: primitive Indians, modern Indian tribes, escaped indentured servants, European settlers of the colonial era, and the present-day residents that live and work the valleys.

The first settlers were Indians. Evidence indicates that very primitive Indians from the Archaic Era resided at the mouth of Seneca Creek. Although some permanent Indian settlement took place in this area of West Virginia, the Seneca area was later primarily used by various tribes for travel and as a hunting ground. The famous Seneca Trail followed the Potomac River, allowing the Algonquin, Tuscarora, and Seneca tribes to trade and make war on each other. As the Indians moved along the trail they must have used the prominent rocks of Champe and Seneca as landmarks. The local legend of Princess Snowbird may be derived from the presence of a band of Seneca Indians that once lived in the area—or it may be the romantic fantasy of later occupants of European descent. While the Indians must have had thousands of years of very fascinating experiences, their lack of recorded history makes our knowledge of that time relatively sparse.

The first European settlers to the region appeared about the year 1746. At that time, West Virginia, then part of what is now Virginia, was the fringe of the great unknown, the American wilderness. The first settlers were preceded by a few mountain men and escaped indentured servants running from Virginia plantations. As time went on, the wilderness rapidly receded to the west.

The American Revolution affected the region as its citizens became embroiled in the conflict and some residents died in the fighting. Various Indian raids slowed development of the region, and on occasion, the European settlers retreated before the Indian attacks. By the time of the Civil War, the Indians had long been driven out of the area.

The Civil War era proved difficult for the residents of Pendleton County. The common belief that the Civil War split families apart was generally true only in border state regions such as Pendleton County. A little over half the county residents were southern sympathizers; the rest were loyal to the North. In this county brother did fight brother, neighbors became enemies, and people were ambushed and killed because of their politics. At the conclusion of the war, the state of West Virginia was carved from Virginia and the residents of the Seneca region returned to a slow and settled rural lifestyle.

Climbing History

The climbing history of Seneca remains almost completely undocumented prior to the year 1939. Of course it has been argued that Indians may have

Don Hubbard traversing under the Cockscomb. (Photo: Paul Bradt)

climbed the South Peak prior to the coming of the European settlers. An early ascent by Indians may have happened, although most evidence from other peaks throughout the United States suggests that these ancient peoples were not greatly interested in climbing difficult summits. It is possible, and maybe probable, that Indians climbed the South Peak of Seneca, but if this occurred it is unlikely that any evidence will ever surface to verify such an ascent. If Indians failed to reach the summit, it is possible that some European settler devised a method of reaching the top of the South Peak. With settlers living almost in the shadow of the cliff it seems reasonable that someone must have explored the cliff to the extent necessary to find one of the easier routes to the top.

Paul Bradt descending from the South Peak. (Photo: Don Hubbard)

Paul Bradt, Sam Moore, and Don Hubbard on the South Peak summit on Easter weekend 1939. The trio made the first traverse of the formation. (Photo: Paul Bradt)

Portion of Tom Culverwell painting made in 1947 showing Seneca climbers Arnold Wexler, John Meenehan (with camera), and Fitzhugh Clark. (Photo: John Meenehan)

The first recorded ascent appears to have taken place in the year 1908. When Paul Bradt, Don Hubbard, and Sam Moore were making their historic 1939 ascent, they discovered an inscription carved on the summit rock: "D.(B). Sept. 16, 1908." It was initially believed that the inscription was left by a surveyor named Bittenger who worked in the region at that time. However, the local family of Joseph Harper reports that Mr. Harper's grandfather, Delmar Harper, climbed to the summit of the South Peak and left his initials, "D.H." The inscription is still visible, but no longer legible. It is possible that Harper climbed either OLD MAN'S or OLD LADIES', names given to these routes much later.

Between 1908 and 1939, climbers made several attempts on Seneca's walls. The late Mr. Buck Harper, Delmar's son and Joe's father, reported

Marian Harvey, Herb Conn, and Jan Conn on the South Peak summit about 1950. (Photo: Conn collection)

that several parties armed with climbing equipment made attempts on the cliff. However, he did not know whether they were successful or what routes they attempted. He also mentioned that his father had made an attempt on the summit during that period.

Herb and Jan Conn are still active in the outdoors. This photo was taken on a hike in South Dakota 50 years after their climbing years at Seneca. (Photo: Conn collection)

A more completely documented climbing history of Seneca Rocks begins in 1935 with a roped descent of the North Peak by Paul Bradt and Florence Perry. Paul Bradt, Janet Mabry, and Bob Gleichman returned in 1938 and worked out a route into the Gunsight from the north side of the rock.

A long Easter weekend in 1939 gave Paul Bradt, Don Hubbard, and Sam Moore the opportunity they needed to climb to the South Peak via an inspired traverse. Their route took in what today are considered many separate climbs and parts of climbs. The group did this ambitious ascent with only three carabiners. Their route took two days to accomplish and followed today's LOWER SKYLINE DIRECT, the last two pitches of SKYLINE TRAVERSE, COCKSCOMB CHIMNEY, the second pitch of WINDY CORNER, and then on up to the summit. From the summit they down climbed to the north as far as they could, then rappelled the East Face. The rappel placed them to the south of the Gunsight in the fading light. Their adventure was capped by a pendulum into the Gunsight followed by a lengthy scramble through the woods. On the way down they met a rescue party racing to save them. They named the entire route SKYLINE TRAVERSE.

After doing GUNSIGHT NOTCH EAST with Jim Lamb in September of 1939, the trio returned in 1940 to record several more first ascents. On this trip they climbed the now fallen GENDARME, GUNSIGHT TO SOUTH PEAK, and a descent of OLD LADIES' ROUTE. The method used for the ascent of the GENDARME is particularly interesting. They repeatedly threw a rope over the top of the pinnacle until it finally caught. They were then able to top-rope the spire. They belayed on the west side of the Gendarme and climbed the east face. Bradt reported the climb to be extremely difficult until Hubbard found an easy line. On Labor Day weekend, 1940, Bradt used the easier line to lead to the top of the pinnacle with Bill Kemper in tow.

During the early 1940s climbers began a slow but steady exploration of the cliff. Prior to World War II, the hardcore Seneca regulars came from either the Washington, D.C., area or Pittsburgh. The Washington climbers were associated with the Potomac Appalachian Trail Club (PATC); the majority of the Pittsburgh climbers were members of either the Pittsburgh Explorers Club, led by Ivan Jirak, or a group known as the Pittsburgh Social Climbers, led by Sayre Rodman.

The sport was far different in its infancy than it is today. Herb Conn, an early Seneca climber, estimates that fewer than 30 climbers a year visited the rocks in the years immediately preceding the war. Travel was difficult and gear scarce. Older Seneca climbers report that in the early 1940s only three carabiners accessible to civilians existed in the entire city of Washington. Climbing teams would seek out easier sections of rock and wander where they could. Prior to the war, routes were not named or rated. An interesting fact was that the majority of the PATC climbers worked for the same employer: most were scientists working with the U.S. Bureau of Standards. The climbers of the 1940s were not like the climbing athletes of today. Most people considered climbers odd. Few of the practitioners ever worked out or trained for the sport, beyond an occasional practice session at nearby Carderock or Great Falls.

*Don Hubbard made an ascent of the South Peak in 1939
and was on the first ascent of the Gendarme in 1940.*

During the war years only a few climbers managed to visit the rocks due to the difficulties created by the war. Government employees worked five and a half days a week, and gasoline rationing prevented travel to the distant Seneca area. Some made the trip on occasion by filling an automobile with climbers and making the drive on long weekends. In 1943–1944, the U.S. Army used Seneca to train mountain troops for action in the Apennines. The 10th Mountain Division held a two-week training camp and taught such useful mountaineering tactics as aid climbing using silent signals and muffled piton hammers. The skills learned by these men were actually used in combat when the 10th Division launched a night attack on an exposed Italian ridge, achieving total surprise. Although most have disappeared over the past three decades, decayed ring angle pitons from their training activities still pepper various routes at Seneca and elsewhere along the North Fork Valley. During their stay the army drove over 75,000 pitons into the cliffs of Seneca, Champe, and Nelson rocks. Unfortunately, many of the army routes were never recorded and have since been renamed. Although most of the army's routes have passed out of memory, they are still noted for two of Seneca's most popular routes, CONN'S WEST and CONN'S EAST.

The original Gendarme climbing store. (Photo: Markwell collection)

The talented Jeff Burns climbing at Seneca before his death in the Tetons. Note the old style gear. (Photo: Bill Webster)

The 1940s ended with a resurgence of climbing at Seneca. Climbers suddenly found themselves rich with equipment. Army carabiners could be obtained from surplus supplies. Prototype army nylon ropes obtained from friends employed by the Defense Department replaced the old heavy 7/16-inch hemp ropes used by climbers for decades. The climbers of the time used thousands of free pitons left behind by the troops. They simply pounded out the pins as needed. Climbers of the late 1940s tended to repeat many of the army routes and often followed lines of fixed pitons up the side of the cliff. During this period the Explorers Club of Pittsburgh prepared the first climbers' guidebook, merely a list of climbs at the rock.

Paul Bradt was probably the first real "hardman" at Seneca. He became a motivating force among the Washington climbers. Using techniques he learned from "Gus" Gambs, a Frenchman employed by the State Department, Bradt climbed many of the first routes at Seneca, Champe, and other rocks. He was also a great caver. He led the first expeditions into the famous Schoolhouse Cave, only a few miles from Seneca. This cave was considered the most difficult cave in the United States for many years. Even today, Schoolhouse is a serious challenge deserving respect. Don Hubbard was another star of the era. Arnold Wexler, a contemporary of Hubbard, described him as a "fantastic climber" who constantly downplayed his own abilities. Hubbard so often stated that he was too old to climb that in 1940 Jan Conn wrote a song poking fun at the supposedly aging warrior. Hubbard made his last Seneca climb in 1983 at the age of 83. On that trip he summitted the South Peak and the Gendarme.

The pioneering climbers of the 1940s who built on the early achievement of Bradt, Moore, and Hubbard were considered to be people with an odd passion. Paul Bradt, Herb and Jan Conn, Charlie Daniels, Don Hubbard, Andy Kauffman, Sam Moore, Chris Scordoes, and others broke the ice at Seneca. Of the core group, only Andy Kauffman and the Conns would go on to receive any degree of fame. Kauffman was known for his mountaineering exploits and the Conns for their many early first ascents all over the United States.

Climbers such as John Christian, Sayre Rodman, Jim Shipley, Tony Soler, Arnold Wexler, and others dominated the 1950s and early 1960s. These climbers increased the quantity and quality of Seneca routes. Some of their better efforts include GREEN WALL, MARSHALL'S MADNESS, SOLER, and TRIPLE S. The ascent of the classic TRIPLE S was notable. Shipley led the steep corner with pitons generally too small for the crack. Perhaps the best climber of the 1950s was Tony Soler. His SOLER ROUTE was incredibly bold for the time. The climb ascends the East Face at its highest point and ends with an exposed traverse to a hidden ledge.

In the late 1960s the number of climbers active at Seneca greatly increased. As more and more climbers made their mark, the number of difficult routes rose tremendously. The climbers of this period had the advantage of better equipment and improved techniques. In addition, competition began to appear at Seneca as a motivating force. These factors allowed the leaders of the Seneca climbing community to concentrate on the creation of hard free climbs. Matt Hale was one of the leaders of this movement. He led the first free ascents of COTTONMOUTH and AGONY. George Livingstone put up the first Seneca route ever given the grade of 5.10 with his lead of MADMEN ONLY (5.10a). COTTONMOUTH and AGONY were both later upgraded to .10a and .10b respectively. Other leaders of the era include Tom Evans, Barry Walden, and Bob Lyon.

The 1970s continued the trend of more and harder routes that began in the late 1960s. In 1971 Pat Milligan and George Livingstone did the twin cracks of CASTOR and POLLUX. John Stannard freed TOTEM and gave Seneca its first 5.11. As the decade progressed, a new crowd began to flex its muscles. The prolific Herb Laeger, most often assisted by Eve Uiga, managed a long list of hard climbs, including CLIMBIN' PUNISHMENT, RIGHT TOPE, HIGH TEST, NIP AND TUCK, and TERRA FIRMA HOMESICK BLUES. Other hardmen of the period included Howard Doyle and Eric Janoscrat, who began climbing many of the less obvious—and sometimes poorly protected—natural lines. Marty McLaughlin, Leith Wain, Ray Snead, Jeff Burns, Hunt Prothro, and Jessie Guthrie also contributed greatly to the first ascent scene.

Ray Snead, John Stannard, and others who were active in past years continued to assist in the development of the area.

The 1980s were an unusually turbulent decade for Seneca. The Seneca community suffered three setbacks: the death of Buck Harper, the fall of the Gendarme, and the great flood of 1985.

Buck Harper, the owner of the Harper General Store and friend to many climbers, died at the age of 74. Mr. Harper was a familiar figure in his bib overalls. At first impression he seemed to be a man who would not inspire friendship from visiting climbers. He often spit tobacco in the general direction of a paint can placed against the stove in his store. Another game that Buck liked to play was "punch me in the stomach." He offered to let climbers hit him in the stomach as hard as they wanted if he could return the favor. He played this game well into his 70s. These antics did not hide the fact that he was an intelligent man who loved to debate the members of the generally more liberal climbing community. His death was a shock to the dozens of climbers who visited Buck's store for many years.

On October 22, 1987, at 3:27 p.m., the Gendarme fell: an event recorded in numerous outdoor magazines. Prior to appearing in print, news of the fall flashed across the country by word of mouth. Someone not familiar with Seneca might wonder at the nationwide attention given to the demise of this little pinnacle. The Gendarme was a special climb. Terribly exposed, it leaned out over the west face. An easy, but airy, 5.4 route followed the east face of the pinnacle to a very tiny, pointed summit. Countless pilgrims arrived at the microscopic, sloping summit to find that vertigo would not allow them to stand up! Since 1940, when Bradt, Hubbard, and Perry made the first ascent, this 25-foot blade of rock was one of Seneca's most popular climbs. Over the years, thousands of people had climbed the narrow pinnacle and stood, or tried to stand, on its summit. No one ever doubted that the Gendarme would go some day. Its deeply cracked base was much smaller than the rest of the pinnacle! The only important question was whether anyone would be on the summit when it toppled. Fortunately it

The Gendarme before the fall. (Photo: Markwell collection)

happened on a weekday, with few climbers around, and no one was hurt. The last known ascent was by local guide Tony Barnes and his client Charlie Reese on October 19, 1987.

On November 4, 1985, this part of West Virginia suffered the worst night of flooding in its recorded history. In one night, the great flood of 1985 brought dramatic changes to the physical environment of the Seneca region. The record floodwaters killed dozens of people and caused millions of dollars in property loss. The losses to the climbing community were minor compared to the tragedies suffered by many local residents. However, some changes to the area stand out. The traditional climbers' camping area along Roy Gap Road was destroyed, as was the old swinging bridge. A bigger campground has been built, and a much larger and safer bridge now spans the North Fork River. Time and money have repaired the physical damage to the Seneca area, but decades of tradition were swept away with the flood in November 1985.

On the climbing front, the 1980s brought another change to the Seneca community. A gradual nationwide acquiescence to sport climbing methods turned into a tidal wave. Seneca has long held a reputation as a crag with many hard gear routes and sometimes difficult protection. At first it seemed improbable that these "Euro" methods would find acceptance at such a traditional area. Prior to 1984, all routes were done from the ground up, including cleaning. After 1984, several hard routes were put up using such methods as rappel-placed bolts and pre-inspection. These routes are located on walls that would have been extremely difficult to climb using ground-up techniques. John Bercaw, one of Seneca's finest climbers, provides an ideal example of the changes that swept the area. In the September/October 1979 edition of *Climbing* magazine, Bercaw published an article entitled "What Price Glory?" In the article he lamented the "disease of impurism." In Bercaw's mind, the disease seemed to be manifested by tactics commonly used today on first ascents in many climbing areas around the country.

Bercaw complained of "aid first tactics, top-roping, or resting on protection." In the article he described the placement of Seneca's first bolt as a defacement of the cliff. Today several hard Bercaw routes, complete with bolts, are found at Seneca.

The change in style and ethics at Seneca was tempered to a certain degree by strong traditional ethics. Today, it is safe to say that most of the hard, new thin-face climbs protected by bolts were drilled on the lead from hooks or marginal pro.

The 1980s brought many 5.12s and one 5.12d/.13a route, FINE YOUNG CANNIBALS. Though the authors of this particular route were not guides, one of the forces behind this movement toward very difficult routes was the founding of the Seneca Rocks Climbing School, and then the Seneca Rocks Mountain Guides. It stands to reason that a "local" population of climbers would develop new and harder routes.

Another driving force in new route development continued to be the dedicated nine-to-fivers from Pittsburgh and other areas in Pennsylvania, the greater D.C. area, and a few other regional population centers.

These young tigers, armed with the best modern gear, skill, and plenty of spare time, put up many excellent hard routes. The activists of the 1980s included Cal Swoager, Paul Anikis, Howard Doyle, John Bercaw, Eric Janoscrat, Eddie Begoon, Pete Absolon, Mike Perliss, Greg Smith, Mike Cote, Mike Artz, Tom Cecil, and Darell Hensley.

In 1981 Cal Swoager completed Seneca's first 5.12 pitch when he freed the first pitch of SATISFACTION #1 (5.12c). John Bercaw introduced Seneca's first 5.13 in 1988, the continuation of Cal's line over the roof. John Bercaw called the completed route FINE YOUNG CANNIBALS. Cal Swoager also free-climbed the fearsome BELL route on the North Peak. Both Jeff Burns and Bill Webster had taken falls in excess of 60 feet while attempting to aid-climb this line in the 1970s.

As the decade progressed, Seneca climbers developed the cliff in two ways; the creation of very hard free climbs with minimal and sometimes nonexistent gear, and the development of face climbs using some rappel but mostly hook-placed bolts. Examples of the former include Cal Swoager's THE BELL 5.12a R; Pete Absolon's SUMMER'S EVE 5.10d X; and Greg Smith's TOTAL MALFUNCTION 5.11c X. Climbs in the latter category include Eddie Begoon's and Mike Artz's MR. JONES 5.11c, John Bercaw's BROTHERS IN ARMS 5.12b, and the Bill Moore–Parker Brothers creation THUNDERBOLTS 5.11d. The number of persons leading and putting up hard new lines was at an all-time high.

The 1990s saw continuing new route activity, most of it involving the use of bolts placed from aid, especially hooks, to which tiny, diamond-hard Seneca features lend themselves particularly well. Tom Cecil, Eddie Begoon, Darell Hensley, Harrison Shull, Chris Tolen, and several others have been hard at work doing routes on the remaining faces, and, with some exceptions, upholding the ground-up style.

In a sad development, the Forest Service Visitor Center building, which had been standing since 1978, burned to the ground on May 26, 1992. It housed irreplaceable natural history specimens and records, as well as prized exhibits.

Finally, in 1999 the new Seneca Rocks Discovery Center was completed.

The rocks have seen generations come and go. The environment, the people, the traditions, and climbing styles have undergone many changes since climbing began at Seneca. The new century has already seen even more change as trails improve and new lines continue to be discovered. The young tigers of today will someday look with awe on the accomplishments of those who follow. It has always been this way, and as long as climbing continues, it will probably remain so.

GEOLOGY

The major cliffs of the Potomac's North Fork Valley in eastern West Virginia, which include Seneca, Champe, and Nelson Rocks, differ significantly from other eastern climbing areas. The rock is similar to the quartzite found in the Shawangunks of New York state and crags in Pennsylvania and Maryland. In the Seneca area, the rock was subject to tremendous geological forces that literally tilted the entire strata on end. Seneca and these other crags are jagged groups of bladelike towers. With its many arches and buttresses, Seneca's South End resembles a fantastic cathedral.

The quartzite in West Virginia is approximately 250 feet thick and is located primarily on exposed ridges as caprock or exposed crags. The rock is formed from sand grains deposited approximately 440 million years ago, in an extensive sheet at the edge of an ancient ocean. About 300 million years ago that ancient ocean was slowly destroyed by continental drift as the area of eastern North America uplifted, thus forming the Appalachian Mountains. These mountains were huge by today's standards, perhaps larger than today's Himalayas. The active geological forces of the era threw the Tuscarora and other rock layers into great folds and zones of sheared rock. Far below the surface, one of the largest of these folds formed a miles-wide arch in the Tuscarora.

Tens of millions of years of erosion stripped away the overlying rock, including the dome of the Tuscarora arch. Fragments of the northwestern wall of the arch remain as Seneca, Nelson, and Champe Rocks. These rocks lie in a straight line northwest and southwest along North Fork Valley. The top and southeastern slope of the arch are preserved on the skyline of North Fork Mountain, whose cliffs of Tuscarora quartzite are visible to the east from Seneca. The cliffs of Seneca remain because their rock is far harder than the surrounding rock. The vertical bedding of the cliff encourages sloughing off of layers, much like an onion. Seneca will be around for a long time, but in the lifetime of the average climber some geologic changes can be seen.

CORRECTIONS AND REVISIONS

Please send corrections and additions to:

Earthbound Sports LLC
P.O. Box 3312
Chapel Hill, NC 27515-3312

GETTING AROUND SENECA

Seneca is a complex cliff that can confuse the first-time visitor. There are two separate summits, numerous walls facing all four main compass directions, many large corners, and several sub-areas. Access to some major sections of the cliff can be difficult if you don't know the tricks. This complexity has resulted in more than a few lost and benighted parties over the years. If you are confused, don't hesitate to ask other parties. (It's rare to find yourself alone at Seneca.) When viewing the rocks from the road, a pair of binoculars is useful but not necessary.

Fortunately, certain aspects of the cliff can help make sense out of a confusing situation. The primary advantage to the first-time climber is that the rocks have an almost perfect north-south orientation. You see the West Face of both summits when looking at the cliff from the town of Seneca Rocks.

WEST FACE OVERVIEW

See the photos on pages 36-37. The freestanding formation of Seneca Rocks is one of the most dramatic-looking climbing areas in the East. This is especially true when seen from the west. Both the spectacular north and south summits are easily viewed from the town below.

One of the most prominent features of Seneca is the Gunsight Notch, the deep saddle between Seneca's two main bladelike summits. This notch splits the wall almost evenly.

As seen from the town of Seneca Rocks, the North Peak–West Face is the entire expanse left of the Gunsight Notch. The Forest Service's Seneca Rocks Hiking Trail, which leads to the summit of the North Peak, switchbacks up the hill to the left of the North Peak.

One striking feature of the North Peak–West Face that cannot be seen until the climber actually stands at the base of the crag is a huge fissure called

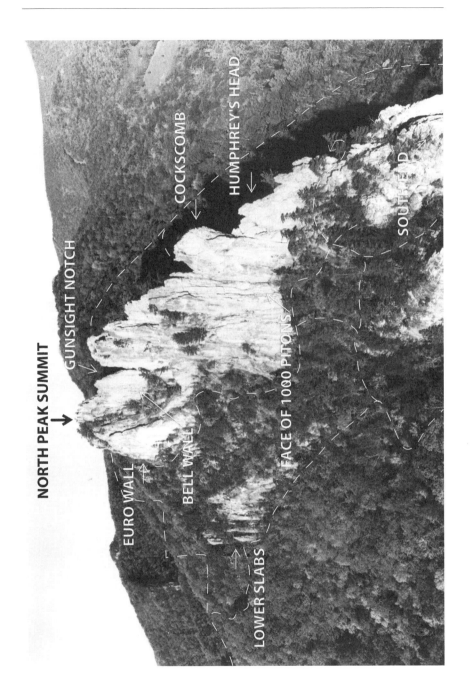

No Dally Alley. The large triangular wall on the far left, known as the Euro Wall, is actually an enormous detached flake that creates No Dally Alley.

To the right of this wall, immediately left of the Gunsight, is the Bell Wall, a steep flat expanse with both fine difficult cracks and good bolted routes. The wall is named for the test piece that goes through the shallow, bell-shaped recess at right center on the wall. All its one-pitch climbs are slightly overhanging and very sustained.

The Gunsight was once the home of an unlikely 25-foot-tall pillar called the Gendarme. (The Gendarme is a latter-day name given the formation by climbers. Since the days of the earliest settlers, locals called it the Chimney). The Gendarme was first climbed in 1940. Until 1987 the spire had one popular 5.4 route and a couple of more difficult and dangerous lines. The pillar was without cracks, except all across the narrow base. It's safe to say that thousands of ascents of the Gendarme were made in the 47 years it was a climbing objective.

The South Peak–West Face is all the rock south (right) of the Gunsight Notch. It is helpful to note the landmarks along the South Peak's skyline. The South Peak rises from the notch as a sharp and sloping arête to the narrow and airy Summit Ridge. It then descends south to Windy Notch, the Cockscomb, Humphrey's Head, and some small unnamed pinnacles. After a short flat stretch the profile plummets down the 200-foot drop of the South End into Roy Gap. Opposite the South End rise the buttresses of the Southern Pillar.

The faces and corners below the skyline create some of the most complicated terrain on Seneca. From left to right, beginning in the Gunsight, the main features are:

> **Greenwall**—This is the bright green wall just right of the sloping arête that forms the right side of the Gunsight.
> **Pleasant Overhangs Roof**—This is the enormous roof that lies directly below the South Peak summit. Can't miss it.

Thais Face—The right side of the Pleasant Overhangs Roof ends at this face, which cannot be seen from the road. It is the right side of an enormous corner, and the longest single feature at Seneca.

Face of a Thousand Pitons—This is another face that cannot be seen from the road. It forms the left side of a huge corner and lies directly below Windy Notch.

Southwest Corner—This is the large triangular wall at the lower right of the face. It lies below the bottom of the main wall and rises from Roy Gap on the northern side of Roy Gap Run. It is topped by vegetated low-angle terrain. This is the first area passed on the West Face Trail.

The Lower Slabs are the less dramatic-looking cliffs located far below the main walls of the North Peak–West Face.

WEST FACE APPROACHES

The following approach descriptions are intended to provide a general overview. More detailed approach descriptions are found in each chapter. Scrambling and short-cutting destroy trails and cause erosion. Please stay on trails marked with blue diamonds or triangles.

Lower Slabs Access

See Approach information in the Lower Slabs chapter on page 41.

West Face Trail

A good trail system provides access to the routes on the West Face, both for the North and South Peaks. Begin in Roy Gap, the chasm between the South End and the Southern Pillar. To reach the West Face, cross Roy Gap Run just west of the Southwest Corner. The blue-marked trail is fairly obvious on the north side of the stream. A massive oak tree fell across the stream in 1991. Follow the trail up steep rock steps to the left of the stump of the great oak. Please stay out of the eroded gully to the right of the stump.

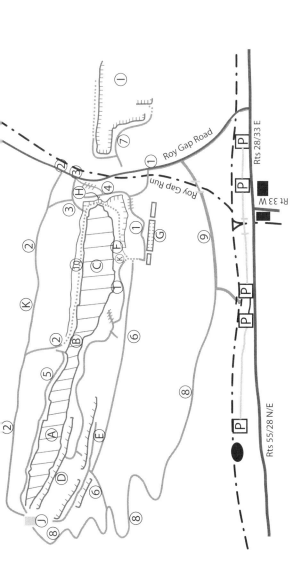

Roy Gap Road

Roy Gap Run

Rts 28/33 E

Rt 33 W

Rts 55/28 N/E

Roads & Towns
Streams
Trails
3rd/4th class
Steps

A - North Peak Area
B - Gunsight
C - South Peak
D - Euro Wall
E - Lower Slabs
F - Luncheon Ledge Area
G - The Block
H - South End
I - Southern Pillar
J - F.S. Viewing Platform
K - Rescue Cache

1 - West Face Trail
2 - East Face Trail
3 - Southeast Corner Trail
4 - South End Trail
5 - North Peak-East Face Trail
6 - Lower Slabs Trail
7 - Southern Pillar Trail
8 - F.S. Seneca Rocks Hiking Trail
9 - F.S. Trail to Roy Gap
10 - Broadway Ledges

CRITTER CRACK

AREA

TRAFFIC JAM

WEST POLE ROUTES

P.O. ROOF

HUMPHREY'S HEAD

COCKSCOMB

OLD MAN'S TRAVERSE LEDGE

FRONT C CORNER

FACE OF A THOUSAND PITONS

LE GOURMET TRAVERSE LEDGE

LUNCHEON LEDGE

THAIS CORNER

Continue to the south edge of a rock fin system standing separate from the main Southwest Corner. This is called the Block. A jog right brings you to wood framed steps. Take these halfway and head left to stone steps in the chasm between the Block and the Southwest Corner. Routes on the Southwest Corner and South End are reached from this portion of the trail.

The stone steps lead into what was once a small flat hemlock grove. Most of the trees are dead or dying from blight. This area will shortly become a small clearing below the talus. Above this the trail ascends about 60 feet of talus to two short 3rd class steps (which may be treacherous when wet or icy). The trail forks in the upper talus. The right branch leads to the base of Humphrey's Head (Luncheon Ledge). The left option leads to the base at LE GOURMET. At this point it traverses north, passing the base of OLD MAN'S and ascending 3rd class steps to the base of the wall beneath the Gunsight, near BANANA. The trail continues to a short scramble below No Dally Alley.

EAST FACE OVERVIEW

The view from the east is only slightly less dramatic than the one from the west. The South Peak looks even more striking from the east. However, the North Peak–East Face is far less imposing than its western flipside.

The Southeast Corner rises from Roy Gap as a triangular face capped by the long Broadway Ledge.

The first major feature that creates the skyline on the left side of the South Peak–East Face is Humphrey's Head. The next major feature to the right is the Cockscomb. Lower Broadway Ledge is located at the base of both formations. Next is the broad and impressive main East Face, which lies above Upper Broadway Ledge. The right edge of the South Peak–East Face sweeps down in a sloping arête into the Gunsight.

Unlike the steep and impressive wall that faces to the west, the North Peak–East Face is a low, broken affair that gradually merges into the hillside north of the formation.

EAST FACE APPROACHES

The following approach descriptions are intended to provide a general overview. More detailed approach descriptions are found in each chapter.

Broadway Ledge From The Roy Gap Area

Do a climb on the Southeast Corner or South End to access the Lower Broadway Ledge.

Broadway Ledge From The West Face

It's common to access the ledge from the west side. Start at Luncheon Ledge, which is at the base of Humphrey's Head. Walk south from Luncheon Ledge and down-climb about 25 feet (4th class) to the left (east) to the south end of Lower Broadway. South Peak–East Face climbs extend north from here. Broadway Ledge can be followed almost into the Gunsight. There are several 3rd class and 4th class steps in the ledge.

East Face Trail

From Roy Gap find the East Face climbers' trail as follows. Follow Roy Gap Road for about 80 feet past the culvert pipe in the Gap and find a blue blaze and signpost at a small cut in the road bank on the left. Walk up and right and find the rest of the Scramble Trail as it follows a low, rocky ridge parallel to Seneca Rocks in a straight climb to a wooded area almost even with the North Peak summit.

Broadway Ledge From The East Face Trail

Hike about halfway up the strenuous East Face Trail. Take a feeder trail (blue arrow and blazes) at a point about even with the Gunsight Notch. Head left (west) to 3rd class and 4th class ledges. After an initial 10 foot rock step scramble left and up about 60 vertical feet to Upper Broadway. The 3rd and 4th class "path" from the end of the feeder to Broadway Ledge follows ledges and steep, must-not-fall terrain (3rd and 4th class), and arrives at the base of CASTOR and POLLUX, two thin, distinctive 5.10 cracks in pale rock.

North Peak–east Face From The East Face Trail

Take the feeder trail described just above and walk across to the rock step. Scramble up at the same point as for Upper Broadway, or 50 feet right at a breakdown in the step. Move right if necessary—all routes start to the right of the Gunsight Notch. The distinctive LICHEN OR LEAVE IT finger crack, though not the first route listed in this guide for the North Peak–East Face, makes a nice reference point. It graces the first smooth wall to the right of the Gunsight, where the climbers' trails reach the base of the wall.

ROY GAP OVERVIEW

The formation on the right side of Roy Gap is the Southern Pillar. For detailed description and approach information see page 141.

The wall on the left side of Roy Gap is the South End. Detailed information starts on page 121.

LOWER SLABS

From the town of Seneca Rocks, the Lower Slabs are visible as the lowest cliff-band below the North Peak. They encompass some freestanding fins on the far left and a long wall of one pitch routes, many of dubious quality and safety.

This area, though completely visible from the road, escaped exploration and development until well after the rest of Seneca experienced intensive new route activity. The prevailing rumor for many years was that the rock was low-angled and loose. Indeed, some Lower Slabs faces do have extensive vegetation and loose flakes, and others are somewhat slabby compared with the rest of Seneca. However, great routes do exist. The less intimidating scale and less strenuous techniques required on some of the more kicked-back climbs offer a refreshing change. Erosion is a very real concern in this area, where trails are steep with little flat or solid terrain. Because of this it is inadvisable for large groups to use this area.

APPROACH

Seneca Rocks Hiking Trail to the North Peak: Routes on the north end of the slabs are best accessed via the 1.7-mile-long Seneca Rocks Hiking Trail, which eventually leads to the observation deck on the North Peak. Hike about halfway up this trail. Continue about 120 yards past the halfway marker, which is on a signpost with an interpretive plaque about iron ore. Instead of following the next switchback left, follow the blue-blazed trail south-southeast into the woods toward the Lower Slabs, below the North Peak. The trail meets the main cliff at SCUTTLE; you'll recognize it by the obvious crack.

From the South Peak: If you are already on the upper Seneca crags, it is best to descend on the West Face Trail to the base of the steep rock steps at the top of the Hemlock Grove talus. Hike north and skirt the base of the short walls that eventually become the Lower Slabs. The first route you will reach is WAP SUCK DIRECT.

DESCENT

It is possible to walk or scramble back around to the base of the routes on the north end of the Slabs. Bushwhacking off from the top of Slab routes farther south is arduous and not recommended. There are no trees, but permanent rappel anchors along the top of the Slabs. If you find it preferable to rappel from your chosen climb, make sure your ropes reach the ground!

Routes 1–4 are located on a detached band of short, smooth walls that lie downhill and north of the prominent Lower Slab cliff-band.

1 FIRE ON THE MOUNTAIN 5.9
Start directly behind an oak tree and just right of a right-facing corner.
#1 Climb the hairline crack that splits the wall.
FA Ron Dawson 1984

2 FOR SLAB RATS ONLY 5.8 G
Walk to the right side of the northwestern–most detached cliff. About 20 feet before the right edge of the cliff, inside an alcove, is a clean right-facing corner on a ledge.
#1 Climb the hand- to finger-sized crack up the corner (40 ft.).
FA Mike Cote, Don Womack

3 DIRTY RAT 5.7
Start 10 feet right of FOR SLAB RATS ONLY.
#1 Climb the crack to two birch trees. Step left to the right-facing corner and then continue to the top.
FA Bill Bechtel, Kristen Behtel 1995

4 ANGRY ANGLES 5.10d R
Locate the pin and bolt on the extreme right edge of the detached cliff.
#1 Climb the fine face and right edge to the top (45 ft.).
FA Greg Smith, Mike Cote
It is advisable to tie off the pin that sticks far out of the rock. There are only two fixed protection points, but they are right where you need them. The

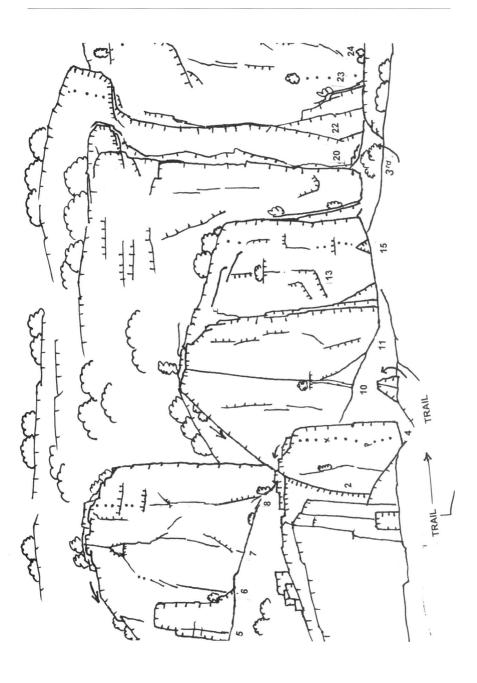

quarter-inch buttonhead bolt needed replacing as of this writing in 2006 (placed circa 1986).

The following Lower Slabs routes, including the best routes in this area, are located just up-slope on the main wall and are described north to south (left to right). The base of this wall shows the effects of foot traffic. Because of loose soils on steep slopes it is inadvisable for large groups to use this area. Routes 5–9 are located to the left of the obvious SCUTTLE crack.

5 PENATOIDAL MEMBRANES 5.7

Begin at the left end of the wall.
#1 Climb the crack and left-facing corner to the top (25 ft.).
FA Eric Janoscrat, Paul Anikis 1982
The narrow right-facing corner is often top-roped.

6 THE WARLOCK 5.9+ PG★

Start at a small tree on a tiny ledge formed by the base of a right-facing flake. This climb is just left of the obvious finger crack of DISCREPANCY and 15 feet right of MEMBRANES.
#1 Climb the thin crack system. Trend right at the top to merge with the more obvious DISCREPANCY (50 ft.).
FA Paul Anikis, Eric Janoscrat 1982

7 DISCREPANCY 5.8 G★

Begin at an obvious finger-sized crack that splits the face at its highest point.
#1 Climb the crack to the top (55 ft.).
FA Drew Bedford, Jim Howe 1981
A Lower Slabs classic.

8 AUTUMN FIRE 5.11c PG★

Start 15 feet right of DISCREPANCY at a very thin crack that slants right to left.
#1 Climb the crack, angling up and left to a small ledge. Climb straight up

the broken face and over a downward-facing flake to the top (60 ft.).
FA Howard Doyle, Paul Anikis

9 DEATH BY ABUNGA 5.9 R
Begin 8 feet left of the obvious SCUTTLE crack.
#1 Climb the face to the top (30 ft.).
FA Paul Gillispie, Chris Guenther, Topper Wilson 1983

10 SCUTTLE 5.7 G★
Start at a prominent vertical crack with a short, wide section. A small tree grows about 10 feet up the crack.
#1 Climb the crack to the large tree at the top (50 ft.).
FA unknown
In order to avoid the first crack, you can start up a narrow ramp just to the left of the normal start.

11 SELDOM SEEN 5.7 PG/R
Begin 20 feet right of the SCUTTLE crack.
#1 Climb the face to a thin, right-facing corner/flake. Continue to a ledge then move right to the base of a narrow left-facing corner and flakes. Follow the system to the top.
FA Mark Thesing, Paul Anikis

12 R2D2 5.5
Start around the corner, 40 feet right of SCUTTLE at two large right-facing corners and a large detached flake.
#1 Ascend the right side of the flake (120 ft.).
FA Jim Lucas, Len Sistek

13 SUMMER BREEZE 5.10b PG
Begin 15–20 feet left of the TIPS flake (a detached blade of rock protruding from the ground inches from the wall) at a right-facing corner formed by two overhangs.
#1 Climb below the small overhang until it is possible to traverse left to

the corner. Undercling 20 feet across the smooth wall. Next, move up and right to a small tree on a ledge. Continue up the corner until it is possible to move right to a large ledge with trees (75 ft.).
FA Chris Guenther, Topper Wilson 1983
Steep, strenuous, continuous, and a little loose at the top.

14 TAPS 5.8 R

#1 Climb up between SUMMER BREEZE and TIPS. Angle toward the top of BREEZE (50 ft.).
FA David Rockwell 1992
Not much gear in the first half; needs cleaning.

15 TIPS 5.10a R

Start at the second wall to the left of the large right-facing corner. Begin at a large, loose, pointed, detached flake that lies only inches from the main wall.
#1 From the top of the pointed flake, move up the face for about 8 feet to an undercling. Move left and up to a small flakey crack. Continue up the crack to a small overhang. Move right and up a small right-facing corner to the top.
FA Howard Doyle, Paul Anikis 1982
Protection is poor and difficult to place. Take plenty of small wired nuts.

16 IT AIN'T THE MEAT, IT'S THE MOTION 5.4 G

Begin around the corner from TIPS at a right-facing corner.
#1 Climb the left side of the corner using cracks and the narrow chimney with chockstones (40 ft.).
FA Rick Fairtrace, Barbara Bates, Cathy Nardini

17 ADRENALINE 5.10a R

Use the same start as SNAKEBITE.
#1 Climb the shallow right-facing corner to an undercling. Climb left and up a short left-facing corner. From the top of the corner, move up and right toward a pine tree and the belay (85 ft.).
FA Paul Anikis, Mike Artz 1983
Take a skyhook.

18 **SNAKEBITE** 5.7

Start to the left of GOOD MORNING at a gully that angles up and left. Scramble up to the second tree.

#1 Climb the flake to the right of the tree until it ends. Move left and climb the wall straight through the small overhangs and up to the pine tree on top (75 ft.).

FA Rick Fairtrace, Glenn Thomas, Barbara Bates

19 **4 ME** 5.4

Use the same start as GOOD MORNING.

#1 Climb the grungy chimney in the right-facing corner. Step out right and pull the small overhang. Continue up the face to the top (80 ft.).

FA Jim Lucas, Len Sistek

20 **GOOD MORNING** 5.7

Begin at the huge, obvious, right-facing corner in the middle of the cliff. This corner can be seen from the road.

#1 Move up the corner past overhanging flakes. Pull the overhang and then continue past a short chimney to a large tree at the top (140 ft.).

FA Eric Janoscrat, Denny McDonough 1977

21 **WITCH WAY** 5.10c

Use the same start as GOOD MORNING.

#1 Climb a large pedestal up the light-colored face. Follow the overhanging crack to the roof. Pull the roof on its right side (50 ft.).

FA Paul Anikis, Eric Janoscrat, Howard Doyle 1982

The protection is good, though difficult to place.

22 **AND GOD CREATED ALL MEN EQUAL** 5.10c **PG/R**

Start underneath the largest roof, just right of GOOD MORNING.

#1 Climb the large, inside right-facing corner to the large overhang. Use horizontal cracks to pull the center of the roof. Continue up a loose, easy, unprotected face to the top (90 ft.).

FA Greg Collins, George Flam 1981

The roof is the length of a small body.

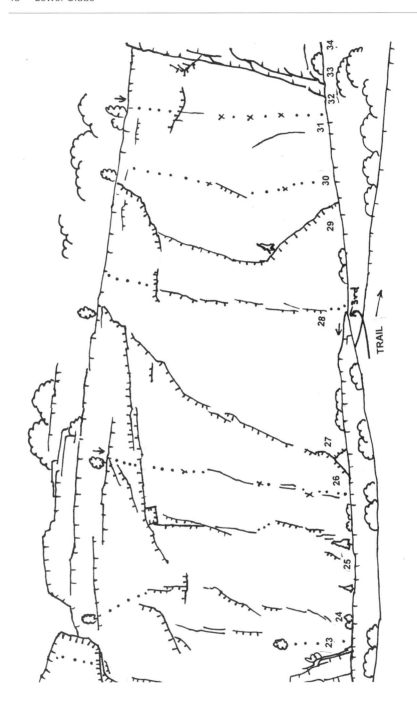

23 **SUNNY DOWN BULOW** 5.9

Traverse right to left under the slabs until past DARK STAR and almost to GOOD MORNING. Cut back south across a ledge to a ramp. Climb the ramp to a spacious ledge. At the left side of the ledge is a right-facing corner with a tree about 25 feet up.

#1 Climb the face just right of the corner. Move past a bush, then traverse right to another right-facing corner. Move up this corner and around to the right of a thin right-facing flake. Move straight up and pass the finish of PRAYING MANTLE (90 ft.).

FA Eric Janoscrat, Howard Doyle, Pannil Jones 1983

24 **PRAYING MANTLE** 5.9

Start just right of SUNNY DOWN BULOW.

#1 Climb up and slightly right on loose flakes to a short, right-facing corner. Move up and over the large flake, past a bush, and into right-facing corners. When the corners end, go up and left to the large pine tree.

FA Eric Janoscrat, Howard Doyle, Mark Thesing 1983

25 **GUILLOTINE** 5.9

Start right of PRAYING MANTLE on the same ledge at a pine tree.

#1 Climb the flake and the short corner. At the end of the corner move left to right-facing corners. Climb up to the gaping, guillotine-shaped rock in the overlap. Climb the left side of the rock and then up right on flakes. Traverse right to a small pine (90 ft.).

FA Howard Doyle, Eric Janoscrat, Lori Larsen, Mark Thesing 1983

26 **THE SECRET GARDEN** 5.10d

Start just left of DARK STAR.

#1 Follow the clean streak through lichen. Climb pass three bolts and use small wires and TCUs to get to the ledge with a small pine (80 ft.).

FA Harrison Shull, Di Botello

27 **DARK STAR** 5.11c **R**

Begin about 80 feet right of the huge right-facing corner at the small alcove that becomes a right-facing corner.

#1 Climb the right-facing corner to a larger right-facing corner. From the top of the second corner traverse up and right under roofs to a pine tree at the top (75 ft.).

FA Paul Anikis, Howard Doyle

The protection is difficult. This condition is compounded by some bad rock.

28 **CAPTAIN HOOK** 5.9+ **R**

Start from a ledge 20 feet left of SENECA SAMURAI.

#1 Move up the face to a right-facing corner and flake system. Pull over the small overhang and then up to the top. (100 ft.).

FA Paul Anikis, Cal Swoager, Eric Thesing, Mark Thesing

This is a good route, though the flake is hollow. Take a skyhook.

29 **SENECA SAMURAI** 5.9

Start from a ledge about 15 feet off the ground and left of a large vegetated left-facing corner.

#1 Climb left to the pine tree. Climb straight up a very shallow corner to the roof. Move right at the roof, then up the corner to the top (80 ft.).

FA Cal Swoager, Eric Janoscrat 1980

30 **KNOW FEAR** 5.10c **R**

There is a bolt to the right of SENECA SAMURAI, a short distance above the ledge.

#1 Climb to the bolt and up to a short, right-facing corner. There is a poor TCU placement in the corner and another bolt near its top (70 ft.).

FA Ed Begoon, Mike Artz, Howard Clark and David Clark 1991

31 **GREEN SNAKE** 5.11a **PG**

Begin 15 feet right of KNOW FEAR and 20 feet left of the vegetated corner. Find three bolts on the face to the right of a left-arching seam.

#1 Climb on thin edges past the three bolts and up to placements for small to medium camming gear. Pull the bulge and continue up easier ground to a tree (50 ft.).

FA Ed Begoon, Tony Barnes 1991

32 **FINGER LICHEN GOOD** 5.6

Start about 15 feet left of WAP SUCK at the obvious layback flake.

#1 Climb the flake. Move up about 40 feet to the end of the crack. Continue up a blocky, lichen-covered face. Turn the corner and finish by mantling a vegetated ledge (45 ft.).

FA Josh Stark, Phil Wilt 1983

33 **WAP SUCK #4** 5.5

At the far right side of the Lower Slabs there is a right-leaning, vegetated corner with a dead tree.

#1 Ascend the right-leaning corner to the top (45 ft.).

FA Eric Janoscrat, Jim McAtee, Bill Lepro 1978

34 **WAP SUCK DIRECT** 5.5

#1 Climb the face to the right of the corner, intersecting the route at its midpoint.

FA Eric Janoscrat, Jim McAtee, Bill Lepro 1978

NORTH PEAK–WEST FACE

The West Face of the North Peak is one of the least-visited walls at Seneca. The reason is simple: the routes tend to be hard, arm-pumping affairs. There are a few easier climbs, but these have relatively long approaches and are often not of the highest quality compared to the easy to moderate routes found at the rest of Seneca. For those who can climb 5.10 and harder, the spectacular cliffs of the North Peak–West Face offer some great routs.

EURO WALL AREA

The Euro Wall is the large face formed by the outside of the huge No Dally Alley flake on the north end of the rocks.

APPROACHES

West Face Trail: See page 34 for a description of the West Face Trail. Follow the West Face Trail to the base of BANANA. Continue walking north (left) on a faint trail until it's possible to scramble up steep, exposed terrain to the base of the middle of the Euro Wall.

Seneca Rocks Hiking Trail to the North Peak: It is also possible to approach from the north by walking up the Seneca Rocks Hiking Trail to a point even with the base of the Euro Wall. From there hike south across rough terrain to gain narrow vegetated ledges leading to the climbs.

Beach Area: Two short climbs may be used to gain a ledge on the far right side of the Euro Wall, dubbed the Beach. Both are on light-colored rock about 40 feet north (left) of the right edge of the Euro Wall. Both have two bolts to shuts; the first bolts are well above the ground. The climb on the left is THE BOARDWALK, 5.8+ PG/R. The one on the right is THE BOATRIDE, 5.11 PG. The easiest scramble is just north of the apex of the roof. An unroped fall on this approach would probably be fatal.

No Dally Alley: Routes are gained via the first pitch of WEST FACE TO GUNSIGHT NOTCH, any of the routes to the right of WFTGN, or by scrambling north from the Gunsight.

DESCENT

Most recent Euro Wall routes are one-pitch climbs with fixed anchors. Use 200-foot ropes. Double ropes can be useful. One can scramble and hike down to the north from the summit of the North Peak.

35 **UP FRONT** 5.3

Start about 50 feet south of and 100 feet below the obscure north entrance to No Dally Alley. This is the leftmost route attainable from the narrow ledges at the base of the wall. It closely follows the left edge of the No Dally Alley Flake formation.

#1 Begin by climbing diagonally left, then right, up a broken, lichen-covered face (70 ft.).

#2 Traverse right 5 feet on a vegetated ledge and then climb a 10-foot crack on the west face, 5 feet north of a left-facing corner.

#3 Scramble up and right to the north end of No Dally Alley.

#4 Climb the north end of the giant flake that forms the Alley. Traverse the top of the giant flake to the chockstone forming a bridge to the North Peak proper (65 ft.).

FA June Lehman, Linda Harris 1971

36 **NAME UNKNOWN** ?

A route up a narrow right-facing corner and the face to the left of SNICKERS was done by Greg Smith and a partner. Details have been lost to the passage of time and other adventures.

37 **SNICKERS** 5.11b **PG**

Begin at a large tree about 60 feet to the left of a large, pointed flake at the center of the Euro Wall. This flake leans into the wall and forms the start of CIRCUMFLEX.

#1 Climb right-facing corners and flakes for about 35 feet. Continue up a small right-facing corner that is somewhat broken. After you pass several pins, the corner ends. At this point traverse to the right about 6 feet to a crack. Continue past several overhangs to a V-shaped notch in the large roof. Pull the roof and move up to a ledge (180 ft.).

North Peak, West Face

FA Jim Marshall, Pete Moore
FFA Howard Doyle, Eric Janoscrat 1978
This route requires a large rack. The first ascent party had to climb in unison due to the length of the route and the absence of ledges. Double 165-foot or longer ropes are recommended. Expect some bad rock and difficult route finding.

38 THAT'S REALITY 5.12a X
Start 15 feet right of SNICKERS.
#1 Climb a nondescript face (5.9 X) to a small right-facing corner about 15–20 feet up. Clip a bolt, then move out and right to another bolt. Continue up to a horizontal crack, and then up past another bolt to a ledge. Continue left to a bolt belay.
FA Ed Begoon, Mike Artz, Kenny Parker 1988
The bolts are difficult to see.

39 THUNDERBOLTS 5.11d PG
Start 15 feet right of THAT'S REALITY, 20 feet left of the large pointed flake at the base of CIRCUMFLEX.
#1 Climb the face past four hard-to-spot bolts. Pull the bulge and move right to gear placements. Continue up the face on the left past four more bolts to the belay.
FA Kenny Parker, Bill Moore, Kevin Parker 1987
This route has eight bolts as well as gear placements. The first bolt is up a bit; the next three are hard to see. Take a #3.5 Friend and tricams.

40 CIRCUMFLEX 5.9 PG★
Start near the center of the west face of the No Dally Alley flake. Scramble to the top of the large pointed flake leaning into the wall.
#1 Climb a line of weakness that splits the face. Move up and right, aiming for the large inverted-V overhangs. Pull the roof just to the right of the apex of the inverted V. Move up to a small belay at the base of a corner (80 ft.).
#2 Climb the corner to the top of the flake. Expect to find loose rock (35 ft.).
FA Dennis Grabnegger, Neil Arsensault 1974

There is a long runout on the wall below the overhang. Several good climbers have logged considerable flight time on this one.

41 **PRINCESS SNOWBIRD** 5.11b **G**★
Begin just right of and below the pointed, detached flake at the base of CIRCUMFLEX.
#1 Climb the face past five bolts to an anchor (85 ft.).
FA Tom Cecil, Eric Anderson

42 **PSYCHO WARFARE** 5.10c **X**
Start at a right-facing corner, 15 feet right of PRINCESS SNOWBIRD and 30 feet right of the large detached flake that marks the start of CIRCUMFLEX.
#1 Climb the right-facing corner to its end. Climb straight up the face to the overhang and the anchors shared by PRINCESS SNOWBIRD. The original finish traversed left for 15 feet and joined with CIRCUMFLEX (100 ft.).
FA Eric Janoscrat, Howard Doyle 1981
The runout to the roof is frightening.

43 **BRAY TO THE LORD** 5.12a **G**
Start to the right of PSYCHO WARFARE.
#1 Climb the face past six bolts to an anchor shared by BRAY NO MORE.
FA Ed Begoon, Howard Clark 1992

44 **BRAY NO MORE** 5.12c **G**★
Start to the right of BRAY TO THE LORD, after scrambling to a point just left of a short right-facing corner in clean rock.
#1 Traverse right into the short corner. Next climb up and slightly left past six bolts to a fixed anchor.
FA Eddie Begoon 1992

The following climbs are below the level of the main Euro Wall ledge and may be used to gain three more climbs on the upper wall.

45 **THE BOARDWALK** 5.8+ **PG/R**

Start 30–40 feet left of the south (right) edge of the No Dally Alley Flake/ Euro Wall, at the base of a clean knobby wall with bolts visible about 12 feet up. This is the left hand of the two routes.

#1 Climb the face past two bolts to a ledge (the Beach) and cold shuts about 25 feet up.

FA Chris Tolin 1999

46 **THE BOATRIDE** 5.11 **PG**

Start just right of THE BOARDWALK.

#1 Climb the face past three bolts to cold shuts.

FA Chris Tolin 1999

Climb THE BOARDWALK or THE BOATRIDE to a ledge directly beneath the next three climbs.

47 **GALILEO** 5.11 **G★**

Start at the shuts above THE BOARDWALK.

#1 Climb slightly left and up past nine bolts to shuts.

FA Chris Tolin, Tom Cecil 1994

48 **NATURAL SELECTION** 5.10 **PG/R**

This is the climb that goes up between the sets of anchors above BOARDWALK and BOATRIDE.

#1 Climb the face past eight bolts to shuts.

FA Chris Tolin 1999

49 **UNDERGROUND PHAT PARTY BLOODHOUND** 5.10 **PG/R**

#1 Climb the face above BOATRIDE'S shuts past nine bolts and gear placements to shuts.

FA Chris Tolin 1999

Bring gear from ½ inch to 1 ½ inches to place between the fourth and fifth bolts.

50 **INHERENT CONTRADICTIONS** 5.10a **R**

Begin near the right (south) edge of the wall, just left of the slightly overhanging 5.6 crack of SECOND TIME. Scramble up 5.0 terrain to a ledge about 25 feet off the ground.

#1 From the ledge, move over the bulge to an inside corner facing right. Climb the corner until you can traverse left toward a small detached column. Climb the face to the right of the column.

FA Howard Doyle, Eric Janoscrat

The route is characterized by difficult protection and loose rock.

51 **2ND TIME** 5.6

This route starts at a slightly overhanging crack immediately left of and below the south entrance of No Dally Alley.

#1 Climb the crack about 40 feet to a good stance. Climb right, around the bulge, to easier rock below an overhanging right-facing corner. Move through the overhang to join with WEST FACE TO GUNSIGHT NOTCH (70 ft.).

FA Bruce Cox, Bob Bock, Al Moore 1982

52 **WEST FACE TO GUNSIGHT NOTCH** 5.0

There is a short face leading to a vegetated ramp at the very lowest point in the wall below the Gunsight. This is about 50 feet left of the point where the West Face Trail meets the wall.

#1 Climb the short wall and follow the ramp up and left to the south entrance of the No Dally Alley chimney (150 ft.).

#2 Scramble back right over ledges to the base of the Bell Wall and from there to the Gunsight Notch.

Above the initial ramp of WFTGN's first pitch is a short, smooth wall with two bolted climbs.

53 **THE WHOLE NINE YARDS** 5.12a

This is the left-hand climb.

#1 Climb the devious, crimpy face past four bolts to cold shuts.

FA Darell Hensley, Brian McCray

54 **OPTIONAL ILLUSION** 5.12b

This is the right-hand climb.

#1 Climb the small, right-facing flake past a horizontal crack, then up the face past four bolts.

FA Ed Begoon 1990

The following three routes are inside No Dally Alley and are listed north to south. These climbs are most easily approached from the south entrance to the Alley. The following approaches can be used: scramble over 3rd class rock north from the Gunsight, climb the first part of WEST FACE TO GUNSIGHT NOTCH, or do a climb to the right of WFTGN.

55 **NO DALLY ALLEY** 5.2

Start inside the No Dally Alley chimney by an area of breakdown near its north entrance.

#1 Follow a ledge on the west wall of the chimney up to the south and climb a short crack to the top of the flake (intersection with KAUFFMAN'S RIB).

#2 Climb up to and over the chockstone bridge to the North Peak proper.

FA John Christian, Ed Worrell, Bill Hemphill 1954

55A **ONE STOP** 5.6 **R/X**

Start about 60 feet inside the south entrance to No Dally Alley.

#1 Stem up the chimney about 60 feet until it's possible to traverse left, on the west wall of the chimney, to a belay ledge on KAUFFMAN'S RIB.

#2 Traverse back into the chimney and take a direct line to the top of the flake. Finish as for the previous routes.

FA John Christian, Ed Worrell, Bill Hemphill 1954

This route is called ONE STOP because there's only one place to quit stemming the chimney, and the FA party moved left to belay at that point. This route takes old-school skill.

56 KAUFFMAN'S RIB 5.4

Begin at the south entrance of No Dally Alley.

#1 Climb the sloping rib south rib of the No Dally Alley flake to its top. Jump the gap to the main rock formation. (140 ft.)

FA   Andy Kauffman and party 1955

A little loose near the top.

57 AMBER 5.10b/c PG/R

Begin about 20 feet inside the south entrance of No Dally Alley on the east (main crag) wall.

#1 Climb a narrow right-facing corner to a ledge 10 feet off the ground. Move up and left to another narrow, right-facing corner and continue over a bulge to the top. Protection is adequate but hard to place at the crux (75 ft.).

FA Howard Doyle, Stan Switala 1993

The following two climbs are to the right of the south entrance to No Dally Alley.

58 MISTAKEN IDENTITY 5.4

Begin outside and to the right of the south entrance of the No Dally Alley chimney.

#1 Move up and right to the base of the left-facing inside corner. Climb the corner until it is possible to move left to a large ledge complete with a pine tree.

59 PINE TREE TRAVERSE 5.0

Begin on the large ledge beneath the Bell Wall.

#1 Climb the vegetated ramp up and left to the summit.

FA Sally Chamberlin, Eleanor Tatge 1946

The following three routes are on the short cliff band above the huge Euro Wall/No Dally Alley flake and are best reached by scrambling down from the North Peak summit.

NO DALLY
ALLEY ↘

56

EURO WALL
↘

56

58

65

60 **PLANET GONG** 5.6 **PG**

Begin at the obvious left-facing inside corner directly below the North Peak summit.

#1 Climb the corner to the ledge (30 ft.).

FA Johnny Robinson, Sandy Fleming, Barbara Fox 1982

61 **FLYING TEAPOT** 5.7 **PG**

Start 20 feet left of PLANET GONG.

#1 Climb the flakes to the ledge (30 ft.).

FA Johnny Robinson, Sandy Fleming 1982

62 **TALK DIRTY TO ME** 5.8 **PG**

Start 35 feet left of PLANET GONG.

#1 Climb flakes to a ledge (30 ft.).

FA Sandy Fleming, Johnny Robinson 1982

BELL WALL AREA

This is the steep, smooth and very intimidating wall between the huge No Dally Alley Flake on the north and the Gunsight Notch to the south.

APPROACHES

West Face Trail: See page 34 for a description of the West Face Trail. Follow the West Face Trail to its high point at the base of the short cliff band directly below the Gunsight Notch. Climb WEST FACE TO GUNSIGHT NOTCH (5.0). It starts 60 feet left of BANANA, where the wall is only about 10 feet high. Or you can do BANANA or another of the short climbs on the initial wall below the Gunsight.

East Face Approach: The Bell Wall can also be reached from the East Face, by climbing into and over the Gunsight Notch from the north end of Broadway Ledge (5.1).

DESCENT

The top of the North Peak in this area is only about 2 feet thick. The old way of descending involved a dangerous traverse of the summit ridge to the north. The danger and inconvenience has been eased by the placement of cold shuts or similar anchors at the top of several routes. A single 200-foot rope or two shorter ropes are necessary for a safe descent. Some climbs on the left side of the wall, such as SILENT BUT DEADLY, are still descended by traversing north along the ridge crest.

63 **SILENT BUT DEADLY** 5.10c **G** ★

Scramble up the chimney at the far left side of the Bell Wall proper until you're atop a ledge that is below and 15 feet to the left of an obvious finger crack.
#1 Climb the crack to the overhang. Traverse left and belay (40 ft.).
FA Howard Doyle, Lotus Steele 1976
Descend by scrambling to the north and hiking off.

64 **HOOKED ON A FEELING** 5.11c **G** ★

Start at a right-facing corner below the obvious slanting, right-facing corner/flake (NEGATIVE FEEDBACK) in the left side of the Bell Wall.
#1 Climb the corner for about 25 feet, until it is possible to clip a bolt. Climb left onto the face and move up past three more bolts to the top and a bolt anchor.
FA Tom Cecil, Sue Hartley 1988
A #2 Rock placement (or equivalent) near the top may be welcome.

65 **NEGATIVE FEEDBACK** 5.11a **PG** ★

This route follows the major right-slanting feature on the left side of the Bell Wall. Start beneath a right-facing corner.
#1 Climb the corner for about 25 feet, to a ledge with a block. Continue up via a right-slanting corner/flake to a notch. Move past the notch onto the face. Move up and slightly right to the top (120 ft.) and a bolt anchor.
FA Jack Beatty, Lieth Wain
Hooks have been used as protection just beyond the last good placements in the corner/flake.

66 NO BOLTS, NO BE 5.12c
This is a hard top-rope problem between NEGATIVE FEEDBACK and SUMMER'S EVE.
FA (TR) Russ Clune 1993

67 SUMMERS EVE 5.10d **X**
Begin 30 feet right of NEGATIVE FEEDBACK.
#1 Climb the shallow left-facing corner up and right to the top.
FA Pete Absolon 1984

68 BANSAI 5.12b **PG/R★**
Start left of MALEVOLENCE at an orange wall marked by horizontals. It's a committing move to the second bolt, as a small (bonsai-like) tree that was slung on the FA has since been broken off.
#1 Climb the face past eight bolts to a cold shut anchor.
FA Tom Cecil, Darell Hensley 1992

69 MALEVOLENCE 5.10c **PG★**
Start about 75 feet right of the NEGATIVE FEEDBACK corner and 60 feet left of the obvious right-facing MADMEN ONLY corner/flake, just to the right of a large boulder.
#1 Climb the crack and face to a small stance at a right-facing inside corner. Move up the corner for about 40 feet to the end of the crack. Traverse right to a second, left-facing corner and then climb straight to the top (100 ft.). Fixed anchors.
FA Hunt Prothro, Charlie Rollins 1974

70 MALEVOLENCE DIRECT FINISH 5.12b
(Var.) Go straight up past three bolts instead of traversing right at the top of the narrow right-facing corner most of the way up MALEVOLENCE.
FA Darell Hensley, Brian McCray 1992

71 **IRRELEVANCE** 5.10d

#1 Climb the first 50 feet of MALEVOLENCE until it is reasonable to move left to an obvious left-facing inside corner. Climb the corner and the face above to the top of the cliff.

FA Jack Beatty, Greg Collins

72 **TOON TOWN** 5.12 ?

This bolted route was unfinished at this writing. The line goes up left of THE BELL and through MA BELL CONNECTION.

73 **THE BELL** 5.12a **R**★

Begin below the bell-shaped arch located high on the wall, midway between MADMEN ONLY and MALEVOLENCE.

#1 Climb the cracks to the base of THE BELL. Continue through the apex of the arch past a corner to a steep face. Ascend the face past a bolt to the top (90 ft.). Fixed anchor.

FA Cal Swoager, Alex Karr, Hunt Prothro, Mel Banks 1983

The first two aid attempts on this route resulted in falls in excess of 50 feet. Everyone on the first ascent was an old man over the age of 30, wearing old-style EB climbing shoes. Serious, scary, and poorly protected.

74 **THE MA BELL CONNECTION** 5.11d

(Var.) Start by climbing THE BELL. Move left before the obvious corner and join with MALEVOLENCE. Finish on MALEVOLENCE.

FA Greg Smith, Andrew Barry 1985

75 **PSYCHO DRILLER** 5.12c★

Begin 30 feet left of MADMEN ONLY.

#1 From the top of a big block, follow the line of six bolts that leads up and left of PSYCHO KILLER. Finish at cold shuts (85 ft.).

FA Tom Cecil 1989

FFA Jim Woodruff

76 **MADMEN ONLY** 5.10a **PG** ★

This climb takes the beautiful right-facing corner/crack just left of the Gunsight.

#1 Climb up to a small stance at the base of the corner. Climb the corner/crack for 60 feet, until it's possible to make moves into the wide crack on the right. Move up and find cold shuts on the right wall outside the crack (80 ft.).

FA Jim Shipley, Joe Faint

FFA George Livingstone, Roger Craig 1966

This was Seneca's first 5.10. The first moves are bouldery and committing.

77 **PSYCHO KILLER** 5.11b **PG** ★

#1 Climb MADMEN ONLY for 50–60 feet to the point where the normal route traverses right. Continue climbing up and left, eventually gaining a shallow right-facing corner. Climb past a bulge, then move up and left to the top (95 ft.).

FA Jack Beatty, Alex Karr 1981

78 **PSYCHO FAGGOTS** 5.11d **R/X**

Begin 15 feet right of the prominent corner crack of MADMEN ONLY, just left of the edge of the wall. This is the first route left of the Gunsight Notch.

#1 Climb the crack and face. Take the upper crack at the split. End at cold shuts (shared by MADMEN).

FA Greg Smith, Mike Cote 1985

(Var.) A variation takes the lower crack (FA Cal Swoager 1985)

SOUTH PEAK–WEST FACE

The South Peak–West Face has more popular routes than any other major wall at Seneca. This face offers classic routes of all grades, from short one-pitch climbs to routes of nearly 300 feet in length. The South Peak consists of all the rock south (right) of the Gunsight Notch, including the Southwest Corner.

APPROACH
West Face Trail: See page 34 for a description of the West Face Trail, which provides access to the entire South Peak–West Face.

DESCENT
It is necessary to either rappel or down-climb 5th class terrain to descend from the upper South Peak. Many climbs have fixed anchors and may be rappelled. Other descent routes require a short walk/scramble to get to fixed rappel routes. Rappel routes go down both the East and West Faces. Most East Face rappel routes go to Broadway Ledge. See the DESCENT description in the South Peak–East Face chapter for a description of these rappel routes. See page 161.

Gunsight Rappel Route
The West Face below the Gunsight can be descended on rappel from the pine with fixed slings and rings on a smooth sloping ledge at the base of the notch itself (85 ft.). An alternative is to carefully climb down 3rd class and 4th class terrain. From the tree with slings, angle north and down about 60 feet to another pine. This one has a crook in its trunk that overhangs the ground. This 35-foot rappel isn't used very much and may lack slings and rings. It is used as a landmark to describe the locations of the next three routes, since it's easily seen from the base of the wall.

In order to descend to the base of the central West Face, use one of the following rappel routes. If you have one rope, three rappels are necessary; two ropes allow you to reach the ground in two rappels. Rappel ropes of 165 feet or longer are recommended.

Conn's West Rappel Route #1

Locate fixed anchors about 10 feet left of the tree mentioned in Conn's West Rappel Route #1. This is a *mandatory* two rope rappel (150 feet) that ends at the anchor near the base of WESTPOLE.

Conn's West Rappel Route #2

This is the original CONN'S WEST rappel rout. From the Summit Ledge scramble down 10 feet (5.0) to reach the pine with slings and rings This tree is at the top of CONN'S WEST DIRECT. From this pine, two ropes (140 ft.) take you to the ledge and rappel tree at the base of WEST POLE, 80 feet above the ground. If you have only one rope, rappel 60 feet from the pine to a ledge with a good-sized birch and a drilled rappel anchor (top of CONN'S WEST chimney/flake pitch). Use caution: this area has a fair amount of loose rock. From here rappel 65 feet and traverse left (north) 30 feet, to the anchors at the base of WEST POLE, 70 feet above the ground.

Old Man's/Neck Press Rappel Route

Begin at the west entrance of the Traffic Jam Chimney, a wide slot near the south end of the Summit Ledge. The rappel route starts at a pair of chained bolts near a largish tree and goes straight down the West Face about 50 feet to two sets of drilled anchors at the narrow south end of the Old Man's Traverse Ledge. From these sets of anchors two ropes reach the ground down the NECK PRESS dihedrals area. If you only have one rope, stop at the cold shuts 65 feet below Old Man's Traverse Ledge at the top of the first pitch of NECK PRESS. These are 70 feet above the ground.

Old Man's/Front C Rappel Route

This rappel route also starts at the Traffic Jam Chimney. Rappel down and trend left (north) over the widest part of the Old Man's Traverse Ledge area to a large pine with slings and rings (55 ft.). With two 165-foot ropes it's possible to reach the ground from this tree, but because of the likelihood of finding climbers below and possible snags, this is not recommended. Instead, rappel from the pine to reach the LE GOURMET TRAVERSE LEDGE (50 ft.). Move about 15 feet left to the pine tree. Rappel from bolts with rings to the ground (95 ft.).

SOUTH PEAK - WEST FACE RAPPELS

A - GUNSIGHT WEST
B - CONNS WEST #1
C - CONNS WEST #2
D - FRONT C - LE GOURMET
E - OLD MANS - NECK PRESS
F - BREAKNECK
G - HUMPHREYS HEAD

*All distances are from anchors to the ground

Access to the Gunsight Notch is blocked by the Banana Wall, an 85-foot cliff directly below the Notch. The next nine routes are located on the wall. Follow the West Face Trail to the base of BANANA, where the trail reaches its highest point.

79 **SHORT STUFF** 5.8 **R**
Begin at a large pine to the right of WEST FACE TO GUNSIGHT NOTCH and about 40 feet left of the crooked pine described just above in the descent information.
#1 Climb the face behind the large pine.
FA Hunt Prothro, Howard Doyle

80 **SCRAMBLED LEGGS** 5.8 **R**
Start right of SHORT STUFF, about 30 feet left of the crooked rappel tree.
#1 Climb the wall to a series of right-facing flakes that starts about 25 feet up the wall (40 ft.).
FA Eric Janoscrat, Jim LaRue, Susan Sands 1979

81 **BODYWEIGHT** 5.9 **R**
Begin 15 feet right of SCRAMBLED LEGGS.
#1 Climb the face beneath the horizontal crack. Move through a broken section and aim for a tiny tree on the face. Pass the tree on its right side, then continue straight up. (35 ft.).
FA Pete Timoch, Bernie Nypaver, Greg Edmonds 1983
Take a complete set of RPs.

82 **NOVA** 5.8 **PG**
Start below the crooked pine used by some parties to rappel from the vicinity of the Gunsight Notch.
#1 Climb the narrow left-facing corner and continue straight up to the pine tree (35 ft.).
FA Chris Kulczycki

83 **LOX** 5.8 **R**

Start directly below the crooked pine.

#1 Climb the roof and face directly to the rappel tree. At the top of the pitch, angle slightly left of the rappel tree (50 ft.).

FA Howard Doyle, Lori Larson

84 **BANANA** 5.6 **PG**★

Begin at the base of the 85-foot wall that guards the western approach to the Gunsight Notch. This is the point where the West Face Trail reaches its highest point, 20 feet to the right of LOX.

#1 Climb the flake to the top (25 ft.).

This popular route has some loose rock in the middle of the pitch.

85 **BANANA DOWN UNDER** 5.6

#1 Climb the first few feet of BANANA until it is possible to traverse left on a ledge. Climb the small left-facing corner to the top.

FA Rick Fairtrace, Kathy Nardini 1983

86 **BANANA PEELS** 5.12b **R**

Begin beneath a piton just right of BANANA. This is at the rightmost of two birch trees and below a series of three horizontal cracks.

#1 Traverse left, then up and left 20 feet, to a flake and crack system. Then go up to the top. The route finishes about 20 feet left of the start.

FA Peter Absolon, Greg Smith

This route was finished with siege tactics. Bring friends, sliders, RPs, small tricams, and double 9-millimeter ropes.

87 **FAT COUNTRY GIRLS** 5.12c **R**

(Var.) Climb BANANA PEELS for 15 feet, then head straight up and out right on the wall past three bolts. End on the DEBBIE/MANUAL DEXTERITY ledge.

FA John Bercaw, Rod Hansen

Routes 88–94 are located on short walls above the nine previously listed climbs and immediately below the Gunsight. The detached left-facing flake 30 feet right of FAT COUNTRY GIRLS is the first pitch of TOMATO.

88 **SLAMLINE** 5.10d **R/X**

Start 35 feet left of and a short scramble below the Gunsight rappel tree.

#1 Climb the face just left of a short vertical crack (20 ft.).

FA Cal Swoager, Drew Bedford 1982

89 **PEDRO'S PROBLEM** 5.10c **G**

This is the short vertical crack mentioned in the previous description.

#1 Climb the crack (20 ft.).

FA Howard Doyle, Lori Larson

90 **BY THE WAY** 5.9 **R/X**

Begin about 6 feet right of PEDRO'S PROBLEM.

#1 Climb the flake system past an obvious horn to the top (25 ft.).

FA Kris Kline

91 **SO WHAT** 5.7 **R**

Start directly behind the small pine tree at the top of BANANA. The route begins at a flake with a piton at eye level, about 15 feet left of the thin cracks of DEBBIE.

#1 Climb the flake and move right for about 20 feet. Move back left and then up a ramp. Follow the ramp to a tree about 25 feet below the Gunsight (35 ft.).

FA Michael Ashe, Jeffrey Hallock 1982

92 **DEBBIE** 5.7 **PG**

Begin 20 feet right of SO WHAT.

#1 Climb thin cracks and flakes to a mantel move that leads to the sloping ledge with the rappel tree in the Gunsight Notch (35 ft.).

A short, enjoyable, but seldom-done pitch.

93 MANUAL DEXTERITY 5.10d R

Start about 15 feet right of DEBBIE and 10 feet left of the bolts of BURNING TENDONS.

#1 Climb the committing face to a finger crack (35 ft.).

FA John Bercaw, Greg Hand

94 BURNING TENDONS 5.12b/c PG

Start 10 feet left of the large left-facing corner that is the second pitch of TOMATO. There is a large tree immediately left of this line.

#1 Climb the steep face past three bolts (80 ft.).

FA Mike Cote, Mike Artz 1986

Take a light rack for the horizontal crack.

The following two classic routes start in the Gunsight Notch and can be accessed from the west by climbing any of the routes from WFTGN to the first pitches of TOMATO and GREENWALL. From the East Face, the Notch can be accessed from the north end of Broadway Ledge via EAST FACE TO GUNSIGHT NOTCH (5.0) or from the ground via GUNSIGHT NOTCH EAST (5.5).

95 GUNSIGHT TO SOUTH PEAK 5.4 G★

Start in the Gunsight Notch, at the base of the narrow, sloping, arête that leads to the South Peak.

#1 Climb the arête toward the South Peak until it is possible to step right to a crack that's actually on the West Face, but very close to the arête. Follow the crack and narrow left-facing corner system to a belay stance with old fixed gear (70 ft.).

#2 Continue up to the right of the true arête to a ledge overlooking the East Face, with the Summit Ridge just above. Watch for loose rock (45 ft.).

#3 Climb up onto the Summit Ridge via its north end and walk, crawl, or slither your way across to the summit register (80 ft.).

FA Paul Bradt, Don Hubbard, Sam Moore 1939

Descend by down-climbing the short low-angled ridge on the south end of the South Summit. This places the climber on the large Summit Ledge. Walk down (south) toward rappel points for both faces. Or rappel directly down the East Face from the South Summit ridge proper. The East Face rappels can be made from the keyhole notch midway along the summit crest, or from bolts on a small ledge just above and to the left (south) of the keyhole notch.

96 GUNSIGHT TO SOUTH PEAK DIRECT 5.5 PG★
Start left (east) of GUNSIGHT TO SOUTH PEAK.
#1 Climb the arête on its east side by using cracks and flakes to bypass the overhanging Gryphon's Beak. Belay at the ledge overlooking the East Face (120 ft.).
#2 Climb up onto the Summit Ridge and finish as in the previous route.
FA Chris Scordoes and party
The cracks and flakes include some poor rock. This, plus sharp edges, make the climb a 5.5 for 5.7 leaders.

MAIN WEST FACE
The majority of the South Peak–West Face routes are located to the right of FAT COUNTRY GIRLS and left of the Face of a Thousand Pitons.

97 TOMATO 5.8 G★
The rightmost feature on the wall below the Gunsight is an obvious detached flake leading to a ledge with a good-sized tree. This is the clean, obvious left-facing flake almost directly under the south side of the Gunsight Notch and several yards to the right of BANANA.
#1 Stem and lie-back the left edge of the flake until you can step over to the tree ledge (40 ft.).
#2 Ascend the large dihedral above the first pitch flake to an intersection with GUNSIGHT TO SOUTH PEAK. Finish on that route.
FA Tom Evans, Matt Hale 1969
An excellent line to the South Summit, with good rock, great position, and a variety of moves.

98 GREEN WALL 5.7 G ★

A smooth white wall covered with green lichen lies to the right of the Gunsight and left of the huge and distinctive PLEASANT OVERHANGS roof. This route climbs the long left-facing corner system that forms the right border of this wall. Start just right of the TOMATO flake at a pair of short left-facing inside corners.

#1 Climb the lefthand corner to gain the ledge. Walk south along the ledge to a decent tree and the base of the corner crack (5.7, 60ft.).

#2 Climb straight up the long left-facing corner past a small overhang and a bulge to a good-sized belay ledge with many loose blocks (5.6–5.7, 110 ft.).

#3 Scramble up and south to the summit (50 ft.).

FA John Christian, Jim Shipley, Alan Talbert 1956

An excellent route on a beautiful face.

99 GREEN DRAGON 5.10a R

#1 Climb the first short corner of GREEN WALL.

#2 From the small tree, climb the black, left-facing corner for about 30 feet, to the roof. Traverse left to a crack. Move up the crack to its end, then climb the face on small holds to the intersection with GUNSIGHT TO SOUTH PEAK (85 ft.).

FA Kris Kline, Eddie Begoon 1983

100 GUNS DO KILL 5.11a PG

#1 Climb the main pitch of the GREENWALL corner to a left-diagonaling crack. Traverse left past one bolt to a left-facing corner. Climb the corner to a small roof. Pull the roof to easy climbing above. Bolt anchor.

FA Graham Dower, Rod Hansen 1993

Two 60-meter ropes are required for the rappel.

101 JADE 5.10a R

Use the same start as GREEN WALL.

#1 Climb the first short corner of GREEN WALL and move south up the ledge.

#2 Drop down slightly and traverse right 15 feet, past the GREEN WALL corner. Move out onto the face to an obvious vertical crack system. Climb

the crack past a bulge and up through two scooped-out areas to a second bulge below a left-facing corner. Climb the corner and continue through a small roof at the top of the corner. Wander up the face to the belay at the end of GREEN WALL (100 ft.).

FA Howard Doyle, Paul Anikis

102 A WHITER SHADE OF PALE A3+

This aid line starts on the ledge atop the first pitch of GREEN WALL, right of center on the Green Wall itself.

#1 Work your way up and left before heading back slightly rightward to the bolts at the top of GUNS DO KILL.

FA Harrison Shull 1999 (solo)

Rack: Brass, nuts, Lowe-balls, SLCDs through 2 inches, lots of hooks (especially Logan flat and bat hooks), rivet hangers, circleheads #0 to #2, heads #0 to #3. There are two rivets, five drilled hooks, many natural hooks, and lots of heading.

103 A BETTER WAY 5.9

Begin near a large tree about 40 feet left of the obvious 250-foot Thais Corner.

#1 Scramble up and left to a ledge. Continue up and left to the top of a ledge system and set up a belay by a small pine.

#2 Climb the lichen-covered face to a dished-out area. Move up a crack system through a bulge. After the bulge, climb the face to a belay near the start of the big pitch of GREEN WALL.

#3–4 Finish on GREEN WALL.

FA Howard Doyle, Mike Whitman 1980

104 PLEASANT OVERHANGS DIRECT START 5.10

#1 Climb the obvious flake that leads to the roof near its midpoint. A bolt was placed just above the flake on the first ascent.

FA Tom Evans 1966

FFA unknown

105 **NOWHERE TO RUN** 5.10 **PG/R**

#1 Climb the first pitch of PLEASANT OVERHANGS until it's possible to reach the base of a left-leaning inside corner. Climb the corner and face to its intersection with PLEASANT OVERHANGS.

FA Howard Doyle, Matt Hale

Protection is "good but hard to place."

106 **DIRECT-TOE** 5.10b **R**

Scramble up and start near the right end of the PLEASANT OVERHANGS roof below an obvious overhanging flake.

#1 Climb the flake that leans right to left. Follow it to the roof about one-third of the way from its right end (60 ft.).

FA Tom Evans 1966

FFA Howard Doyle, Matt Hale

Protection is difficult to place on the steep sections.

107 **PLEASANT OVERHANGS** 5.7 **PG**★

Start 30–35 feet left (north) of the tall, north-facing Thais Face.

 #1 Climb either blocky, left-facing flakes up the face, or the dirty left-facing wide crack with a chockstone (not recommended). Aim for a steeper corner with flakes and some poor rock below the very right end of the huge roof. Belay at a small ledge at the intersection of the roof and the obvious 200-plus-foot north-facing Thais Face. This ledge has some old fixed gear (5.7 PG, 100 ft.).

#2 Make thin-face moves off the ledge and begin to move up and left under the huge roof. Near the end of the roof, place gear for your second and make a delicate step or two down and left to a hanging belay (5.7, 70 ft.).

#3 Pull the bulge just above the belay and follow the left-facing, left-trending inside corner up to easier terrain and a ledge. There is some poor rock (5.7, 75 ft.).

#4 Scramble up to the summit (5.0 and exposed, 50 ft.).

FA Jim Shipley and party

The first pitch area is greasy when wet, run out, and a tad loose into the bargain. The first 100 feet of THAIS DIRECT may be used as an alternate first pitch for this exciting, out-there moderate. Bring a few large (3 ½ to

5-inch) pieces. You need two 60-meter ropes to reach the ground from the rappel bolts found near the top of this route.

108 ARRESTED MENTAL DEVELOPMENT 5.9+ PG

Start several feet above the usual belay at the end of the second pitch of PLEASANT OVERHANGS.

#1 Move up and traverse the right wall of the PLEASANT OVERHANGS third pitch corner, past a piton and onto the West Face, above the roof. Move up the face past a bolt to thin cracks. Climb the cracks to the top.

FA Tom Cecil, Tony Barnes 1988

109 ALEX IN WONDERLAND 5.12a PG

#1 Climb the first pitch of PLEASANT OVERHANGS.

#2 Traverse out under the huge roof until just left of center.

#3 Pull the huge 15-foot roof. Traverse right 25 feet to good pins. Climb the crack to the top.

FA Alex Karr, John McKigney 1982

110 P.O. DIRECT FINISH 5.12b PG

#1 Climb the first pitch of PLEASANT OVERHANGS.

#2 Traverse out under the huge roof to the midpoint.

#3 Pull the roof.

#4 From the pocket on the face, climb the face above to a bolt. Climb the face to the right of the bolt, then regain the crack. Follow the crack to the top.

FA Eric Janoscrat, Jim Lucas 1977

FFA Alex Karr

This was an old aid line from the 1970s.

111 THE SORCERER 5.11a PG

Start at the top of the first pitch of PLEASANT OVERHANGS, or use THAIS DIRECT to reach the same spot.

#1 Pull the lip near the right end of the PLEASANT OVERHANGS roof and climb the face above past four bolts and gear placements.

FA Tom Cecil, Chris Clark 1992

Bring a rack up to 2 ½ inches.

112 **THAIS DIRECT** 5.7 **PG**

Begin at the base of the huge Thais Corner.

#1 Climb the crack and ledges in the back of the corner to the ledge at the right end of the PLEASANT OVERHANGS roof. There is some old fixed gear here (100 ft.).

#2 Continue climbing the corner, but do not finish straight up the corner. After reaching a ledge on the West Face, move up and left for about 20 feet to a gully/ledge below the summit (110 ft.).

Bring a few large (3 ½ to 5-inch) pieces.

In 1972, a Fritz Wiessner route, THE BUTTRESS FINISH, was destroyed when the entire upper left section of the Thais Face fell to the ground.

113 **THAIS** 5.6 **PG**★

This justifiably popular route climbs the tall, narrow north-facing (right) wall of Thais Corner.

#1 Start roughly in the center of the wall at a short left-facing corner (there are variations). Head for a good ledge at the base of the prominent chimney (85 ft.).

#2 Climb the 40-foot cavelike chimney, then step left and climb along a crack and arête to a small ledge. Belay left of a smooth, gray corner with a thin crack (85 ft.).

#3 Traverse left to the THAIS DIRECT corner crack. Move up and then left to a ledge on the main West Face (90 ft.).

(Var., 5.8): Instead of traversing left at the start of the pitch, climb the piton-studded crack past THAIS ESCAPE (see below) and continue up thin cracks and more old pins before moving left to the THAIS DIRECT corner.

#4 Follow the ledge north on the West Face, pass a tree, and then scramble to the summit (45 ft.).

FA John Christian, Bob Hinshaw 1954

John Christian explained that the route is named after Thais, a prostitute in the opera of the same name. After failing to seduce a monk, she repented and vowed to follow a "straight and narrow" path.

THAIS FACE

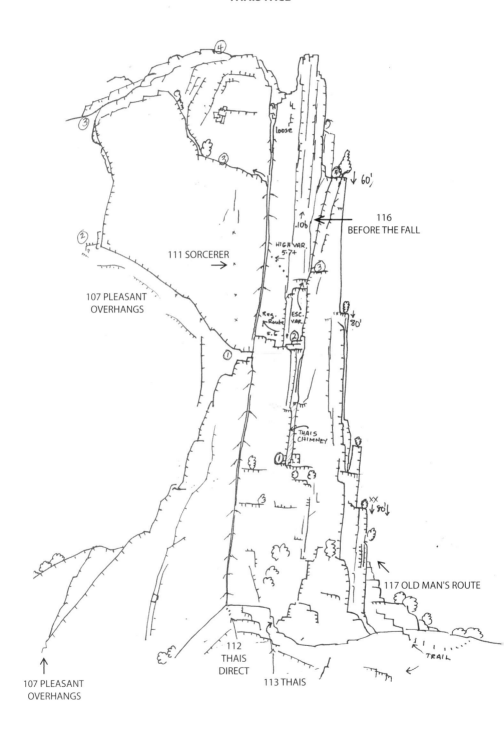

107 PLEASANT
OVERHANGS

114 **THAIS ESCAPE** 5.5 **G**★

#1 From the belay at the end of the second pitch of THAIS it is possible to climb up the piton-studded crack about 10 feet. Move right to the base of a low-angled ramp and corner on the West Face. Move up 30 more feet and belay (45 ft.).

#2 Finish up the ramp and corner to the belay/rappel tree shared by WEST POLE and CONN'S WEST DIRECT (50 ft.).

FA John Christian, Jim Shipley 1956

An airy line with variety and good rock.

115 **DRESSING ROOM** 5.11c **PG**

Begin just below the south summit, at the large undercut area located right of the top of THAIS.

#1 Pull the double-tiered roof to the top (25 ft.).

FA unknown

FFA Greg Smith 1987

Heads up for loose rock! **G** if it all stays put.

116 **BEFORE THE FALL** 5.10b **PG**★

Start on the ground right of THAIS.

#1 Stay right of THAIS and climb up somewhat unprotected but easy terrain to a ledge with a tree (70 ft.).

#2 Climb the crack right of the THAIS chimney. Step left and climb the face of the column past a bolt to the level of the top of the THAIS chimney. Climb up a second column right of THAIS, then move left across THAIS ESCAPE to a thin crack in a corner. Climb 12 feet to a small belay ledge on the left (100 ft.).

#3 Climb straight up the wildly exposed north edge of the fin above THAIS (50 ft.).

FA John Kelbel, Dan Caston 1997

Much of the lower part of this route had been climbed as variations of THAIS, but the upper part is a fantastic journey. The second ascent party suggested a middle belay at the THAIS ESCAPE ramp for a two-pitch route.

117 OLD MAN'S ROUTE 5.3 PG★

Start to the right of the huge Thais Corner on the main West Face, at ledges leading up and right.

#1 Scramble up the ledges, aiming for a left-facing inside corner with a narrow 10-foot chimney, just below a tree. Climb this wide crack to a large ledge (100 to 120 ft., depending on where you belay).

#2 Climb the next short chimney to the beginning of the Old Man's Traverse Ledge (25 ft.). It is also possible to climb a few feet to the right of the chimney, along a 3-inch crack in a blocky wall.

#3 Walk south on Old Man's Traverse Ledge to a point near its end, in a group of small trees (85–95 ft.).

#4 Scramble up and right over ledges and flakes to a large, vertical corner. Climb the corner (crux) past an old fixed pin and pull over the chockstone to the top (50 ft.).

#5 Walk through the obvious horizontal chimney (Traffic Jam Chimney) to the Summit Ledge. Follow the broad ledge north to the final summit scramble. Rope up if necessary.

FA Pim Karcher, Ken Karcher, Dick Gaylord, Bob Tieman 1949

At times this popular route is the scene of traffic jams. The end of the last pitch is also one of the standard rappel routes for the South Peak. At the start of the route, about 15 feet above the ground, remember not to climb too far to the right, as this will place you off route on LE GOURMET TRAVERSE. False moves to the left at the 100-foot point on the first pitch will put you off route on CONN'S WEST.

118 BRING ON THE NUBILES 5.9+ PG★

This route starts 80 feet above the ground (use the first pitch of OLD MAN'S ROUTE), 2 feet left of the WEST POLE belay/rappel anchors, near the arête formed by the intersection of the main West Face and Thais Face. It climbs spectacular rock directly to the top of a sharp fin that's level with the South Summit.

#1 Climb short cracks up the face to an inverted V notch. Climb through the overhang, then step left. Continue up to the THAIS ESCAPE ledge and belay (5.8 PG, 100 ft.).

#2 Climb thin cracks in the West Face straight up to a small stance. Move up and right to thin horizontal cracks. Follow the cracks until you're on a blank face. Move left here (crux), then climb up and slightly right to easier ground and the summit. Continue to the top (90 ft.).
FA Hernando Vera, Kevin Stephens 1985
This may be the last significant Seneca route to go all clean—no bolts or pins.

119 **LOLITA** 5.11a **PG**
Begin on the same face as the second pitch of BRING ON THE NUBILES. Start to the right of NUBILES at the start of the obvious WEST POLE DIRECT FINISH crack. The top CONN'S WEST rappel tree is found here.
#1 Climb a few feet up the right-facing flakes, then trend left along a seam and use finger pockets to climb the face.
FA Pete Absolon
Bring micronuts.

120 **WEST POLE** 5.7+ **G**★
Climb most of the first pitch of OLD MAN'S ROUTE, then move left to a large ledge. Belay at or near the rappel bolt just to the left of and below trees and obvious double cracks.
#1 Follow the double crack system up and then slightly right, to a belay below the large double overhang (70 ft.).
#2 Climb the crack directly through the double overhangs. At the top of the second roof, climb a left-facing corner to easier ground. Move up and right, aiming for the obvious rappel tree at the top of CONN'S WEST DIRECT (65 ft.).
FA George Bogel, Jim Payznski 1970
FFA Tim Beaman, Larry Myer 1971
An excellent route that sports an imposing roof of only moderate difficulty. The route is easier than it appears from the ground. Some parties do this as one long pitch.

121 WEST POLE DIRECT FINISH 5.8 G

#1 There is a prominent crack and right-facing corner to the left of the belay/rappel tree atop CONN'S WEST DIRECT. Climb this to the top (50 ft.).

FA Joe Ebner, Dennis Grabnegger, John Markwell

Bring some big gear for a short fist and off-width section.

122 SOLIDARITY 5.9

(Var.) Use the same start as WEST POLE.

#1 Climb the first pitch of WEST POLE.

#2 Climb the second pitch of WEST POLE through the first roof. Traverse out left 20 feet and then up 50 feet to a belay.

123 GRANDIOSE 5.6

(Var.) This is a traversing line that connects WEST POLE with CONN'S WEST. Climb WEST POLE for about 50 feet, then traverse right, past CLARKE'S CLIMB, across the face to the belay (35 ft.).

FA Joe Faint, Jim Shipley

124 CLARKE'S CLIMB 5.9 G

Begin to the right of small trees and large blocks that mark the start of WEST POLE.

#1 Climb the vegetated offwidth crack formed by the left-facing corner past several small trees and bushes to a point below the right side of the WEST POLE roofs (70 ft.).

#2 Move out right and up the wall to the West Face. Move up to the small tree above (25 ft.).

#3 Diagonal up and left to the last pitch of WEST POLE (25 ft.).

FA Clarke, D. Kepler 1972

125 CLARKE'S CLIMB DIRECT FINISH 5.7

(Var.) Instead of moving back to the WEST POLE line, continue straight up the face to the tree.

FA Ron Walsh, Bruce Cox 1981

126 DAYS OF FUTURE PAST 5.8+ R

#1 Climb the flake-covered face directly between CLARKE'S CLIMB and CONN'S WEST. Belay at a stance just right of the WEST POLE roofs.

#2 Climb up to the rappel tree. The direct route under the tree is 5.11 R/X and an old TR problem; veer left for more humane terrain.

FA Harrison Shull, Dave Cox late 1990s

Some terrain is shared by BY-PASS.

127 CONN'S WEST 5.4 PG★

The start is the same as OLD MAN'S ROUTE.

#1 Climb OLD MAN'S ROUTE until you are directly below a big, obvious, left-facing corner/chimney/flake. This is the CONN'S WEST flake. It lies to the right of the offwidth corner of CLARKE'S CLIMB.

#2 Climb to the base of the corner/flake by climbing the OLD MAN'S chimney for 10 feet, then moving left. Or climb the short, steep corner directly below the big flake (5.5). Continue up the corner/flake to a blocky ledge with a large tree and a pair of rappel bolts (60 ft.). There are dangerous quantities of loose rock on these ledges.

#3 Scramble up and right through the gully. Climb past several large chockstones to the top. A short rappel or scramble down to the south is needed to reach the Summit Ledge area (75 ft.).

FA N. C. Hartz, Henry Schulter, Earl Richardson 1944

Use caution and helmets. There have been frightening instances of rockfall loosened by climbers on the ledge at the top of the second pitch.

128 CONN'S WEST CORNER START 5.7 G

Start between the CONN'S WEST corner/flake and the start of the OLD MAN'S Traverse Ledge.

#1 Climb the nice dihedral with the two trees growing out near the base.

#2 Continue up CONN'S WEST chimney or CONN'S WEST DIRECT. There is some loose rock.

129 **BY-PASS** 5.7 **PG**

(Var.) Start at the corner/flake pitch of CONN'S WEST.

#1 Climb the main corner of CONN'S WEST for about 25 feet, until it is possible to angle up and left toward the roofs of WEST POLE. Continue to work left and up and belay on the THAIS ESCAPE ramp (100 ft.).

#2 Climb a crack to the sloping ledge above, then move right and finish on WEST POLE DIRECT FINISH.

FA John Markwell, John Christian, Arnold Wexler 1972

130 **CONN'S WEST DIRECT FINISH** 5.5 **G**★

(Var.) From the end of the middle corner/flake pitch, avoid the huge chimney by climbing the large right-facing corner above and to the left of the large tree (60 ft.).

FA Arnold Wexler

131 **OUT OF THE COLD** 5.10d **PG**

(Var.) Climb the incipient cracks and face immediately right of CONN'S WEST DIRECT FINISH.

FA Pete Absolon, John Govi 1984

132 **IRONY** 5.5

(Var.) From the top of the corner/flake pitch of CONN'S WEST, climb the gully for 10 feet then go straight up to the ledge. Follow the left-facing corner to the top.

FA Pete Absolon, Linda Elleson

The next six routes start at the base of the cliff.

133 **APRICOT** 5.4

Start about 30–45 feet right of and below the OLD MAN'S start, just right of a large overhanging root system for two birch trees 8 feet above the trail.

#1 Climb the weakness in the face straight up to small ledges and the Le Gourmet Traverse Ledge (80 ft.).

FA John Christian, Tony Sanders 1997

134 **MONKEY SEE MONKEY DO** 5.9 **PG**

Start on the ground 45–60 feet to the right of and slightly below the base of the OLD MAN'S start.

#1 Climb left-facing flakes and a small corner to a more prominent left-facing corner. Pull a bulge with orange rock (bolt and piton) to a ledge. Follow a crack off the ledge to the Le Gourmet Traverse Ledge.

#2 Climb the wide crack formed by right-facing flake. Angle up and right via a thin corner and cracks. At a bolt move 5 feet right and gain the corner to Old Man's Traverse Ledge.

FA R. D. Smith, Paul Fomalot 1998

135 **PRUNE** 5.7 **PG**★

Start where the West Face Trail first meets the crag, about 75 feet right of the base of OLD MAN'S and 75 feet left of prominent arêtes (base of LE GOURMET). Find a left-facing flake at about head level.

#1 Climb the flake and face to a low-angle section that soon steepens. Climb the clean face past small ledges to the Le Gourmet Traverse Ledge (100 ft.).

#2 In a direct line with the first pitch, climb cracks and blocks on the steep wall to a narrow ledge. Follow a leaning finger crack (crux) through a clean wall to a large pine on the OLD MAN'S Ledge (100 ft.).

#3 Move right and climb the right-facing edge of a huge flake until it is necessary to step left. Continue up and right past finger cracks to a good belay on a flat ledge with a good hardwood tree and cracks (60 ft.).

(Var.) A good variation moves just left from the belay at the top of the second pitch (on Le Gourmet Traverse Ledge) and climbs the left-facing corner formed by the huge flake described in pitch #3. Move right and rejoin the regular third pitch.

#4 Climb the left-facing corner above the tree ledge to a huge flake. Follow the edge of the flake to the top (50 ft.).

FA John Christian, Arnold Wexler 1971

To descend, either rappel or down-climb the south-facing chimney topped by blocks with rap slings. Guard against ropes getting stuck. The nondescript first pitch has caused route location problems. It is a bit run out and tricky to protect. The narrow ledge below the second-pitch crux has caused many ankle injuries. Protect frequently as you climb the thin crack.

136 CAST OF THOUSANDS 5.10a R/X

Begin approximately 30 feet right of the start of THE PRUNE, almost directly beneath the prominent rappel tree on Le Gourmet Traverse Ledge. #1 Scramble up and climb the wall straight up to the right side of the roof. Traverse left about 8 feet, until it is possible to pull up onto the steep white face. Climb the face to the Le Gourmet Traverse Ledge (70 ft.). #2 Climb FRONT C to the vegetated platform of OLD MAN'S ROUTE (40 ft.). #3 Scramble up and left to the leftmost of three large pine trees on OLD MAN'S ROUTE. Climb straight up a thin crack 8 feet right of the tree to a left-facing corner. At the top of the corner move right, then up to a belay at the base of the chimneys on the last pitch of LE GOURMET (35 ft.). #4 From the tree, step out left onto the lichen-covered face. Follow the thin crack up and left to the base of a right-facing flake. Climb the flake and the face to the top (50 ft.). FA Bill Webster, Jay Hutchinson 1979 The first pitch is the best, but also the one rated R/X. Other people involved were Bill Lepro, Sayre Rodman, Mark Thorne, Chris Lea, etc., etc.

137 FRONT C DIRECT 5.9 R

Begin just right of the first pitch of CAST OF THOUSANDS. #1 Climb a hard-to-protect face up to a right-facing corner left of the LE GOURMET corner. Take the corner to the ledge (90 ft.).

138 LE GOURMET 5.4 PG★

Start at the area where the left fork of the upper West Face Trail arrives at the base of the rock; here the cliff forms a large arête and south-facing corner. On the West Face, just left of the large arête, find a short, easy corner leading to a long, north-trending ledge. #1 Climb the corner 15 feet and traverse north to the base of a longer corner. Belay or climb 45 feet up a steep corner to the Le Gourmet Traverse Ledge and belay at bolts. #2 Traverse right from the tree and climb diagonally to the outside corner of the south-facing LE GOURMET DIRECT START wall. Climb this arête to the vegetated ledges at the north end of the Old Man's Traverse.

Protection here is less than stellar and may warrant a PG rating (100 ft.).

#3 Scramble up and left behind a large 4th class flake to the base of the prominent south-facing chimneys at the left side of the clean, 50-foot Critter Wall (60 ft.).

#4 Climb the rightmost chimney and corner cracks to the top (75 ft.).

FA Larry Griffin 1965

To descend, rappel or down-climb the south-facing chimney topped by blocks with rap slings. Guard against ropes getting stuck.

139 LE GOURMET TRAVERSE (4th class)

This is a prominent ledge that splits the face from the vicinity of the base of OLD MAN'S ROUTE to the top of the first pitch of LE GOURMET. It affords an easy escape from several routes.

The next nine routes start from the Le Gourmet Traverse Ledge.

140 THE PEACH 5.8+ R

Begin on the Le Gourmet Traverse Ledge, 30 feet left of FRONT C and 5 feet right of a thin flake system.

#1 Climb up a short wall to a small roof. Climb the roof, then continue up the wall, eventually heading slightly right. Follow good holds straight up the wall to the left-facing corner. Continue to a ledge.

FA Howard Doyle, Eric Janoscrat, Paul Anikis 1982

The protection is poor at the crux but improves higher up.

141 THE PLUM 5.9 X

Start on the Le Gourmet Traverse Ledge, about 10 feet left of FRONT C.

#1 Climb the short wall to the right-facing corner. Climb past the corner to a short left-facing corner. Climb the corner and the wall above to a tree (75 ft.).

FA Eric Janoscrat, Howard Doyle, Paul Anikis 1982

Eric Janoscrat reported that climbing this was akin to gambling with your life.

142 **FRONT C** 5.6 **G**★

At the top of the first pitch of LE GOURMET, directly behind the pine tree on
Le Gourmet Traverse Ledge, there is a prominent, curving left-facing corner.
#1 Follow the corner up to the ledges at the end of the OLD MAN'S
TRAVERSE ledge (50 ft.).
FA Sayre Rodman

143 **HISHIRYO** 5.12C **R**

Start 10 feet right of the FRONT C corner.
#1 Climb the face to the left of the bolt. Make a dynamic move to the
bottom of the crack. Climb the thin crack for a couple of moves, then reach
left to a finger crack. Climb the crack to a ledge.
FA John Bercaw, Rod Hansen
This thin line requires micronuts.

144 **RONIN** 5.12d **R**

Begin a few feet right of HISHIRYO, just left of the slightly more obvious
thin cracks of PROJECTED FUTURES.
#1 Climb the face to a bolt and piton. Move right into a finger crack. Climb
the crack to Old Man's Traverse Ledge.
FA Mike Artz
FFA John Bercaw, Bill Dimsdale
Bring along micronuts for this one as well.

145 **PROJECTED FUTURES** 5.12b **R**

Start 50 feet right of the FRONT C corner, to the right of the bolt and pin
of RONIN.
#1 Climb clean rock to the crack that starts about halfway up the face.
FA Pete Absolon
Bring many small brass or steel nuts. Double ropes are helpful.

146 **EASY OVER** 5.5

(Variation to LE GOURMET) From the middle of the traverse on the second pitch of LE GOURMET, it is possible to climb straight up through an S-shaped crack to the vegetated ledges at the north end of the Old Man's Traverse Ledge (90 ft.).

FA Chris Schenk, Mark Reid 1975

The following routes start either from the upper OLD MAN'S Ledge, or are on the Critter Wall near the top of the third (4ᵗʰ class) pitch of LE GOURMET. The Critter Wall is located between the fourth pitch of LE GOURMET and the last pitch of OLD MAN'S.

147 **A THOUGHT FORGOTTEN** 5.10c PG

Start two-thirds of the way south along the Old Man's Traverse Ledge, left of a large tree at a high point with small boulders.

#1 Climb a short, right-facing corner, then move left and pull a small roof and bulge. Continue up to the top (100 ft.).

FA Seth Murphy, Ian Boyer 2002

There is one bolt. You will need at least one #0 TCU.

148 **BACK TO THE FRONT** 5.9 **PG**★

Use the same start as A THOUGHT FORGOTTEN.

#1 Move up and right to a bolt, then continue past one more bolt and two fixed pitons (100 ft.).

FA Dan Miller 1993

Take a standard rack.

149 **CRUSHER CRITTER** 5.9– **PG**

Start on the Old Man's Traverse Ledge at a short smooth wall 30 feet below the Critter Wall proper. It begins about 20 feet right of BACK TO THE FRONT and around a small corner.

#1 Climb the finger crack past a loose block. Finish at the start of CRISPY CRITTER (30 ft.).

FA Greg Collins, Hernado Vera

The next 5 climbs start on a narrow tree ledge 30 feet above CRUSHER CRITTER and the OLD MAN'S Ledge.

150 **CRITTER CRACK** 5.6 **G**★

Start 2 feet right of the base of the fourth pitch of LE GOURMET, which is a large chimney.

#1 Climb the hand crack close to a block at the left side of the wall. (The last pitch of LE GOURMET will be to your left.) Continue up the hand and finger crack to the top (45 ft.).

FA Dave Garman, Mike Murphy, John Markwell 1972

151 **CRISPY CRITTER** 5.7+ **G**★

Begin 10 feet right of CRITTER CRACK.

#1 Climb the thin crack (50 ft.).

FA Gary Aiken, Charlie Fowler

152 **POOR MAN'S CRITTER** 5.7

(Var.) Climb CRISPY CRITTER until it is possible to step left to another crack. Follow the crack to its end (50 ft.).

FA Gary Aiken, Steve Piccolo

153 **CURLY CRITTER** 5.9 **R/X**

Begin just right of the other Critter Wall cracks at an old pin about 4 feet off the small ledge.

#1 Follow a hairline crack to the top.

FA Cal Swoager, Bruce McClellan 1981

154 **KOSHER KRITTER** 5.10d **PG**

Start from a narrow ledge left of the Traffic Jam Chimney at the top of OLD MAN'S ROUTE.

#1 Climb the face past a bolt to a left-leaning crack.

FA Mike Perliss, Peter Absolon 1983

Micronuts are needed to protect the moves to the bolt.

155 **KOSHER KRITTER DIRECT** 5.9+ **PG**

(Var.) Start on the Old Man's Traverse Ledge and climb the face directly below KOSHER KRITTER. Two bolts protect the smooth face. Finish on KOSHER.

FA Howard Clark, E. Begoon, Rick Fairtrace, Amy Clark, Tracy Ramm

156 **TRAFFIC JAM** 5.7+ **G★**

Begin at the south-facing, inside wall of the chimney at the top of the last pitch of OLD MAN'S ROUTE.

#1 Climb the clean crack that splits the white, south-facing wall of the chimney (45 ft.).

Though short, this is a classic pitch. It may be a little easier if you stem the back wall.

157 **LOW RISE** 5.7

#1 Climb the wall directly opposite TRAFFIC JAM. The edge is off limits (25 ft.).

158 **ROAD KILL** 5.7

#1 Climb the short face and crack 10 feet right of the TRAFFIC JAM/ OLD MAN'S belay tree.

FA Ron Dawson, Les Newman, Rick Scott

The following four climbs start from the ground to the right of LE GOURMET.

159 **THE BITE** 5.9 **R/X**

Begin at the start of LE GOURMET, left of and just around the corner from LE GOURMET DIRECT START.

#1 Climb straight up steep, shallow right-facing corners to join a ledge with a pine tree (75 ft.).

#2 Continue straight up the face to the large ledge (30 ft.).

FA Chris Rowins, Chris Kulczcke 1979

160 LE GOURMET DIRECT START 5.6 PG★

This popular pitch climbs the south-facing wall of the huge inside corner right of LE GOURMET.

#1 Climb left-of-center up the south-facing wall. Cracks to the right are 5.8. The line goes to the right of one small tree and left of the second. Belay on Old Man's Traverse Ledge. Beware of rope drag, poor communication, and loose rocks at the top (130 ft.).

#2–3 Finish on LE GOURMET.

This route is somewhat awkward and harder than it looks.

161 NECK PRESS 5.7+ G★

Begin at the base of the west-facing wall of the large dihedral of LE GOURMET DIRECT. This is 20 feet left of a large outside corner.

#1 Climb the slightly curving, right-facing dihedral that lies a few feet left of a small roof. At the top you will find steep, awkward moves that lead to a sloping ledge with a small tree and a bolt anchor (65 ft.).

#2 Step left and climb the back of the corner. You will encounter a strange off-width section and hand cracks near the top. Belay on the ledge, which is also used as a main rappel station at the south end of the Old Man's Traverse Ledge (65 ft.).

#3 The last pitch follows clean cracks in a corner to the right of the last pitch of OLD MAN'S ROUTE (60 ft.).

162 SIDEWINDER 5.11a PG★

Begin 10 feet right of NECK PRESS and about the same distance left of the huge outside corner taken by COTTONMOUTH, at a small right-facing corner capped by a roof.

#1 Climb the corner to the roof. Pull through the roof and move up the face until it's possible to make a scary traverse left to cold shuts, which are shared by NECK PRESS and a rappel route (65 ft.).

#2 From the right edge of the belay ledge, climb straight up to a small roof. Surmount the roof and follow a small diagonal crack to a left-facing corner. Climb the corner and belay at the tree and bolts at the end of Old Man's Traverse Ledge. (65 ft.).

FA Howard Doyle, Eric Janoscrat

163 **THE VIPER** 5.12b **PG**

(Var.) Climb the second pitch of SIDEWINDER through the bulge. Continue diagonally up and right, past a flake and thin crack, left of the bolts on BLACK MAMBA. Climb past a fixed pin to the top.

FA Pete Absolon, Topper Wilson 1986

164 **BLACK MAMBA** 5.12a **PG**

(Var.) Start at the top of the first pitch of SIDEWINDER.

#1 Climb through the first bulge on the second pitch of SIDEWINDER and move up and right toward a face with three bolts. Make a short traverse right at the second bolt and climb up past another bolt and right-trending seams to the anchors on VENOM (70 ft.).

FA Tom Cecil, Ed Begoon 1992

Bring small TCUs and micronuts.

165 **COTTONMOUTH** 5.10a **PG**★

This route ascends immediately left of the outside corner of the Face of a Thousand Pitons, in shallow right-facing corners.

#1 Climb a short, narrow dihedral until it is possible to move left to another corner. Climb up through the steep, orange-colored rock to right-facing flakes and a small ledge. Belay at cold shuts (90 ft.).

#2 Step out right onto the Face of a Thousand Pitons and climb up to the MARSHALL'S MADNESS belay ledge on the outside corner. Belay at cold shuts.

#3 Move right and climb up cracks on the left side of the Face of a Thousand Pitons and belay at cold shuts (45 ft.).

FA Tom Ramins

FFA Matt Hale, Tom Evans 1969

Pitches #2 and #3 (5.8) are easily combined. This great, hard, old-school free climb was rated 5.8 for many years. It then progressed to 5.9 in quintessential denial of an expanding YDS rating scheme. Most people wish for a little more protection that can be placed from less arm-blowing stances.

Emil Briggs on MARSHALL'S MADNESS (5.9). (Photo: Bill Webster)

166 **VENOM** 5.10b **G**★

#1 From the belay at the top of the first pitch of COTTONMOUTH, step left and climb the right-facing corner/flake to the belay of MARSHALL'S MADNESS (65 ft.).

#2 Move out left onto the West Face to reach a thin crack that splits the smooth wall. Follow the crack through the lichen to the top (65 ft.).

FA Hunt Prothro, Herb Laeger, Charlie Rollins 1975

FACE OF A THOUSAND PITONS

The Face of a Thousand Pitons is the tall, narrow, south-facing wall forming a 100-foot dihedral at the north edge of the Cockscomb. It was named many years ago in memory of the training undergone by infantry troops under the guidance of the 10th Mountain Division during World War II.

167 **MONGOOSE** 5.10d **PG**

Start just right of COTTONMOUTH on the south-facing side of the arête.

#1 Climb the finger crack near the corner of the Face of a Thousand Pitons.

FA Eddie Begoon, Pete Absolon

168 **MARSHALL'S MADNESS** 5.9 **G**★

Near the left side of the Face of a Thousand Pitons is an obvious hand- and fist-sized crack system. Start on the large ledge beneath the face, or from down on the ground.

#1 Climb the steep cracks past a small overhang, to a hanging belay stance at cold shuts (40 ft.).

#2 Continue up steep, wider cracks until an easier traverse to the left is possible. Belay on the airy ledge on the outside corner of the face at cold shuts (75 ft.).

#3 Move back toward the right and climb easy cracks and chimneys to the top. Belay at cold shuts (50 ft.).

FA Tom Marshall, John Christian 1955

Some parties combine some or all of the pitches.

FACE OF 1000 PITONS

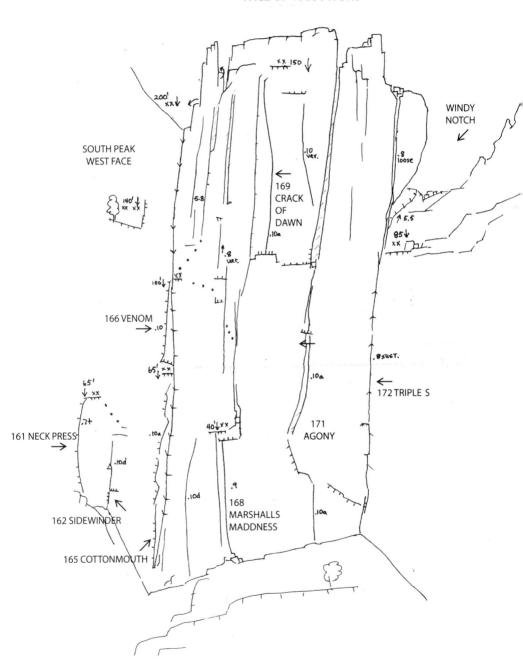

Climber on CRACK OF DAWN (5.10a). (Photo: Bill Webster)

169 **CRACK OF DAWN** 5.10a G★

#1 Climb the first pitch of MARSHALL'S MADNESS (40 ft.).

#2 Climb the second pitch of MARSHALL'S until it is possible to move right to a small overhang. Climb the beautiful jam crack through the overhang and up the face. The crack splits the face located between AGONY and MARSHALL'S MADNESS (120 ft.).

FA Marty McLaughlin, Eric Janoscrat 1980

One of the best routes at Seneca. Yes, the arête is on route. Cold shuts at the top allow a 165-foot rappel back to the base.

170 **HORRENDOUS TRAVERSE** 5.7

#1 Start from the top of TRIPLE S and drop down about 15 feet. Traverse left across the Face of a Thousand Pitons to the small COTTONMOUTH ledge on the west corner of the face. The traverse is about level with the chockstone on AGONY.

#2 Continue traversing north on a small ledge to the large ledges of OLD MAN'S ROUTE.

FA John Christian, Bob Hinshaw 1959

FFA unknown

171 **AGONY** 5.10b **PG**★

About 15 feet left of the TRIPLE S corner is an obvious crack/chimney system that splits the center of the wall. Begin on the large ledge just left of the start of TRIPLE S.

#1 Climb directly up a very thin crack to gain the main cracks. Climb the cracks to the overhang. Pull the overhang to a very uncomfortable belay in the narrow chimney (90 ft.).

#2 Climb the narrow chimney to the top (90 ft.).

FA George Livingstone, Tim Schenkle

FFA Matt Hale, Bob Lyon 1968

The short but difficult direct start was done by John Stannard in 1971. The original route traversed in from the right.

172 **TRIPLE S** 5.8+ **G**★

The left side of the West Face of the Cockscomb and the right side of the Face of a Thousand Pitons form a beautiful, steep corner. Start below the corner on a large ledge.

#1 Climb the corner to cold shuts at a ledge below Windy Notch (85 ft.).

#2 To finish, either climb straight up the DIRECT FINISH or climb up and right to the last pitch of WINDY CORNER (5.4).

FA Jim Shipley, Joe Faint 1960

This highly recommended route was originally named SHIPLEY'S SHIVERING SHIMMY.

173 **TRIPLE S DIRECT FINISH** 5.8 **G**

(Var.) This is the crack directly above the regular route (50 ft.).

FA Chips Janger, Matt Hale 1968

Watch for loose rock.

THE LUNCHEON LEDGE AREA

The Luncheon Ledge is located at the south end of the South Peak–West Face. It is a meeting and staging area that is commonly used by classes and beginners. The next 14 routes are located on the prominent curved pinnacle known as the Cockscomb, located between the Face of a Thousand Pitons and Humphrey's Head. Humphrey's Head is located directly above Luncheon Ledge and is probably the most popular area for beginners.

174 TOTAL MALFUNCTION 5.11c X

Start just right of TRIPLE S.
#1 Climb the face to Windy Notch (100 ft.).
FA Greg Smith, Mike Cote 1985

There are a number of ways to descend the Cockscomb. If you climb to the very summit of the pinnacle you can rappel the west face from a very small tree using two ropes. However, because of the diminutive size of the tree it may be safer to traverse off to the north to Windy Corner.

175 BREAKNECK 5.7 PG/R ★

This climb follows the obvious left-facing feature in the middle of the west face of the Cockscomb. Start at the center of the West Face of the Cockscomb, below a small birch tree.
#1 Climb the short low-angled face to the tree. Traverse up and right until below a huge left-facing flake. Or scramble to Luncheon Ledge and traverse left to the base of the huge flake. Climb just left of the flake for 50 feet, until it's necessary to lie-back a wide crack. Thin face moves on the left are also possible. Belay just behind or on top of the flake (5.6, 100 ft.).
#2 This pitch has been called BREAKNECK EXTENSION. Climb the flake a short distance. Follow a crack that starts easy but thins. Make unprotected 5.7 moves to the top of the Cockscomb.
#3 Traverse north and climb down into Windy Notch. Continue on WINDY CORNER.
FA Ivan Jirak

176 JANKOWITZ-KAMM 5.5 G

(Var.) #1 Stop before the end of the first pitch of BREAKNECK and belay behind the flake near fixed slings. Follow a crack system up and left to Windy Notch (80 ft.).

#2 Finish on WINDY CORNER.

FA Jerry Jankowitz, George Kamm

Watch for loose rock.

177 BREAKNECK DIRECT 5.10b PG★

This route follows the vertical crack on the West Face of the Cockscomb, about 20 feet right of BREAKNECK.

#1 Climb the first 20 feet or so of BREAKNECK, then step right to a thin crack. Follow the crack nearly to its end. Move right a few feet and continue up the face to the ledge with a tree. Cold shuts are located left of the tree (80 ft.).

FA unknown

FFA Jeff Burns 1974

This route can be done with a 5.10 PG direct start. This variation is commiting and requires the use of micronuts.

178 HIT THE SILK 5.11 R

Begin 15 feet to the right of BREAKNECK DIRECT.

#1 Climb the steep face. Eventually tread slightly left to a thin crack. Climb the crack to a ledge with a tree and shuts shared by BREAKNECK DIRECT (85 ft.).

FA Rob Robinson, Robyn Erbesfield 1984

Bring double ropes, a double set of RPs, tricams, and small TCUs.

179 PARTIAL CANOPY 5.11 R/X

Start right of HIT THE SILK, just left of the edge of the south-facing HEARTBURN chimney/flake.

#1 Climb the face trending slightly left to very thin cracks. Climb these to the top and move left to a ledge with a small tree and cold shuts (85 ft.).

FA Greg Smith, Andrew Barry 1985

Bring thin gear, including micronuts.

180 **HEARTBURN** 5.6 **G**

The wide crack on the right margin of the west face of the Cockscomb can be used to make the start of COCKSCOMB PINE TREE a little more exciting.
FA Thais Weibel, George Livingstone 1967
Take at least one #4 Friend or other similar large gear.

181 **OLD LADIES' ROUTE** 5.2 **G**★

Begin on the Luncheon Ledge, at the gap between Humphrey's Head and the Cockscomb.
#1 Climb up through the notch between Humphrey's Head and the Cockscomb. Belay on a flat ledge with a view to the east. Or initially belay on the west side of the notch for convenience, then move the belay prior to doing pitch #2 (90 ft.).
#2 Move out onto the East Face by climbing right and then down. After one exciting move, begin traversing right on an easy ledge to several large trees. There is also a high version that allows the leader to protect the second: traverse right from the belay and step over to a narrow left-facing corner and good handholds. Finish the ledge traverse (75 ft.).
#3 Climb up and right to the north end of the ledge and climb the sloping flake/chimney (100 ft.).
#4 Walk right on the large Summit Ledge for about 100 feet to the final Summit Ridge. Many people simply scramble up the exposed 4th class section to the summit. If you are unsure of your ability, belay the final exposed section to the actual summit.
This is the easiest climb to the summit of the South Peak. On busy weekends this route is usually very crowded.

182 **FOGHORN LEGHORN** 5.9 **R**

Start from the first pitch of OLD LADIES', at the south edge of the huge flake that forms Cockscomb Chimney.
#1 Stay directly on the arête and climb past a serious, runout section to a belay just below the level of PINE TREE TRAVERSE.
#2 Continue up the arête, past a spectacular finish, to the top.
FA Brian Rennex, Sandy Fleming 1986

183 **COCKSCOMB PINE TREE** 5.4 **PG**★

Start as for OLD LADIES'.

#1 Climb to a stance about 10 feet up in the notch between Humphrey's Head and the Cockscomb. Stay left and climb a narrow slot to the base of the huge Cockscomb Chimney. Climb up over a large, awkward chockstone and then up into a niche at a cleft in the huge flake that forms Cockscomb Chimney (5.3, 80 ft.).

#2 Climb a crack leading up and slightly left onto the open west face of the Cockscomb. Belay on a narrow rubbly ledge. This was, until 1999, home to a tall dead pine, hence the name of the route (5.3, 40 ft.).

Believe it or not, the original route climbed *a piton ladder in the tree* to the top of the Cockscomb. Now you can't do that, so see pitch 2 of BREAKNECK, or do the following:

#3 This pitch was originally done separately and called COCKSCOMB PINE TREE TRAVERSE. From the ledge at the end of the first pitch of COCKSCOMB PINE TREE it is possible to make an easy but spectacular traverse straight across the top of the Cockscomb to the Windy Corner notch. Good protection is sparse (5.4, 60 ft.).

184 **COCKSCOMB CHIMNEY** 5.5 **R**

#1 Climb halfway into the chimney, then head straight up past a left-facing flake to the chimney's top.

#2 Move to the narrow, rubbly ledge (which formerly held a dead pine) as discussed in the previous route.

185 **COCKSCOMB OVERHANG** 5.6 **R**

#1 From the end of the chimney, climb over the top of the right (south) side of the huge flake that forms Cockscomb Chimney. Continue to the top of the Cockscomb.

FA Paul Bradt, Sam Moore, Don Hubbard 1939

FFA unknown

186 **COCKSCOMB OVERHANG DOUBLE DIRECT** 5.11d **R/X**

#1 The south face of the Cockscomb proper is a narrow overhanging wall. Climb the left side of the face via thin, shallow cracks just right of Cockscomb Chimney.

FA Greg Smith, Pete Absolon 1984

187 **COCKSCOMB OVERHANG DIRECT** 5.9+ **PG**★

Start at the prominent block at the top of the first pitch of OLD LADIES'. The route ascends the South Face of the Cockscomb to the right of COCKSCOMB OVERHANG DOUBLE DIRECT.

#1 Climb the overhanging crack to the overhang above. Pull through the overhang and continue up easier rock to the summit of the Cockscomb (100 ft.).

FA Mike Nicholson 1967

This route has been the scene of more than one major incident. To avoid a hard runout section, move left when the main crack ends. Take a few pieces from 3 ½ to 4 ½ inches.

188 **HUMPHREY'S HEAD, West Face** 5.3–5.7 ★

Usually top-roped. The most southerly of the prominent pinnacles on the skyline of the South Peak is Humphrey's Head. Many easy routes ascend this small summit where countless beginners have had their first rock-climbing experience. Luncheon Ledge is located at the base of Humphrey's Head's west face. Either down-climb the north ridge (5.0) or rappel (60 ft.).

SOUTHWEST CORNER

This is the massive triangular corner that lies below and south of the Main West Face.

APPROACH

Top of the Corner: Routes 189–192 begin on a rock mass that caps the Southwest Corner. There are two ways to get to these routes. Here's the first option: you can climb ECSTASY JUNIOR, then scramble and hike north about 75 yards, then down and back south along the base. The second

Typical weekend crowd on the Luncheon Ledge below Humphrey's Head. (Photo: Bill Webster)

option is easier: this approach is via the West Face Trail. See page 34. From the Hemlock Grove, about ¾ of the way up to Luncheon Ledge, walk right a short distance. The first route reached is ORGANICALLY INCLINED.

West Face Trail: See page 34 for a description of the West Face Trail, which provides access to the remainder of the Southwest Corner routes.

189 **ORGANICALLY INCLINED** 5.9

Near the extreme north end of the Southwest Corner, about 30 feet south of the Hemlock Grove, is a relatively large, right-facing corner. Start at a thin crack about 5 feet left of the corner.

#1 Climb the crack to its top. Step right, then continue up the crack and face to the top.

FA unknown

FFA Pete Absolon, Topper Wilson 1983

190 **FLYING CIRCUS** 5.9

Start about 40 feet right of ORGANICALLY INCLINED at a wall with two arches.

#1 Climb the two lowest overhangs. Follow the shallow lefthand crack to the face above. Continue straight up to the large tree that grows next to the boulder (75 ft.).
FA Mitchell Wood, John Campbell, Sean Maisel 1981

191 THE HANG 5.7

Start near the center of the right arch.
#1 Start on the crack that leads up to the double overhang. Pull both overhangs, then over a third. Belay at a large pine tree.
FA Mitchell Wood 1981

192 BOTTOM TORQUE 5.9+

Begin at the south end of the overhangs capping the Southwest Corner, at an area of low-angle slabs several feet right of THE HANG. Begin about 2 feet left of a rusty old piton that lies hidden in an overlap about 6 feet off the ledge.
#1 Follow the crack straight up through the overhang. Traverse left and up to an opening in an overhang. Climb the overhang and crack, then move up and over a third overhang. Belay at the pine tree (75 ft.).
FA Mitchell Wood, John Ross 1981

The following climbs ascend the lower Southwest Corner from the scree and talus chasm taken by the main West Face Trail. The first, GERT'S GRUNGY GULLY, ascends a major vegetated, left-leaning gully about halfway up the chasm.

193 GERT'S GRUNGY GULLY 5.0

Start about 150 feet uphill of the southwest corner of the formation. Begin at a tiny cave at the base of a vegetated, right-facing, left-leaning gully.
#1 Climb up and left through the obvious gully (150 ft.).
FA Gert Christie

194 WIFE'S A BITCH 5.9+ R

#1 Climb the first portion of GGG.

#2 Climb a right-facing corner 25 feet to an overhang. Pull the overhang. Continue up another right-facing corner to the top (75 ft.).

FA Ed McCarthy, Paul Gillispie, Kenny Hummel

This pitch goes up about 15 feet left of THE CON MAN. The protection is very sparse above the roof.

195 DIRTY HAIRY 5.6 R

#1 Climb the first 75 feet of GERT'S GRUNGY GULLY to a good ledge. Climb a right-facing flake to the roof. Step left and over the overhang. Run it out to the top.

FA Mike Whitman, Lori Larson 1980

The pro is good to the roof, but there is nothing above.

196 THE CON MAN 5.9 PG

Begin just left of VEGETABLE VARIATION and right of GERT'S GRUNGY GULLY at the obvious wall below the DIRTY HAIRY variation.

#1 Climb the short, but obvious, left-facing corner to a ledge, or climb the first pitch of GERT'S GRUNGY GULLY (50 ft.).

#2 Begin at a short right-facing corner with a tree. Climb straight up the wall, through a roof and up the face above. Climb through a second roof with a cleft. Continue through a third roof (125 ft.).

FA Howard Doyle, Eric Janoscrat, Paul Anikis

197 MR. NO WRENCH 5.11d PG

Go up GERT'S GRUNGY GULLY to a good ledge below the large roof of ROOF TRAVERSE. This route is left of the second pitch of ECSTASY JUNIOR.

#1 Follow the smooth face past bolts up to the roof. Crank over the roof and up the face above to a two-bolt anchor.

FA Ed Begoon, George Powell, Tom Cecil 1993

Carry a few medium-sized nuts.

198 **B&B** 5.10 **R**

Start on the same ledge as MR. NO WRENCH.

#1 Climb the face right of MR. NO WRENCH (left of the second pitch of ECSTASY JUNIOR) to intersect ROOF TRAVERSE at its right end. Finish on ROOF TRAVERSE.

FA Ed Begoon, Ben Bullington 1987

199 **ECSTASY JUNIOR** 5.4 **PG** ★

The start is the same as for GERT'S GRUNGY GULLY. Move right to the tree ledge that comes in from the right about 15 feet up. Some people scramble to this point to rope up and belay, while others start from the ground. Another starting point is from the flat area at the top of the wood steps. Climb straight up the vegetated ramp to the tree ledge mentioned above.

#1 From the tree ledge, move up and right past another tree. Continue right on a foot traverse. After 10 feet or so, follow an obvious vertical crack through a bulge and up to the large tree-covered ledge (70 ft.).

#2 Climb the large right-facing corner to a small overhang. Climb past the overhang and the small cave to a steep face. Climb the crack and face to the top (80 ft.).

FA Chris Scoredos, Don Jacobs, Roy Britton

An interesting route of moderate nature. Steep but reasonable.

200 **VEGETABLE VARIATION** 5.4

(Var.) From the top of the first pitch of ECSTASY JUNIOR, move left to a vegetated crack. Climb the crack to the top (100 ft.).

201 **ROOF TRAVERSE** 5.7

The start is the same as ECSTASY JUNIOR.

#1 Climb up and right on ECSTASY JUNIOR for about 10 feet, to a steep right-facing corner. Climb the corner, then step left to an easy vegetated crack. Follow this crack to the tree that lies next to the large roof. (The continuation of the crack is VEGETABLE VARIATION.) Traverse out right beneath the roof. When the overhang becomes double-tiered, pull the roof to a right-facing corner. Follow the corner to the top (60 ft.).

202 **LICHEN NEVER SLEEPS** 5.9

Use the same start as ECSTASY JUNIOR.

#1 From the large pine tree, traverse straight right until just short of the large crack. There is a small roof overhead, after short right-facing corners. Climb straight up to the difficult-looking crack that comes out of the roof. Climb up to the ledge (60 ft.).

#2 Climb straight up the wall using a left-facing flake about 25 feet right of the right-facing corner of VEGETABLE VARIATION. Merge with ROOF TRAVERSE (80 ft.).

FA Eric Janoscrat, Barbara Bates, Rick Fairtrace

203 **MOONSHINE** 5.11d **R/X**

(Var.) Climb the face just right of the vegetated ramp that begins ECSTASY JUNIOR and lies just left of SUNSHINE. Join the regular route just below the bolt.

FA Mike Cote, Mike Artz 1986

Bring a #0.4 TCU and some brass or steel microwires for the desperate lead. Usually top-roped.

204 **SUNSHINE** 5.10a **PG**★

Begin at the center of the flat area above the wooden steps.

#1 Climb the thin face and cracks to a bolt. Climb past the bolt to an overlap, then up a clean white face and finger crack to the ECSTASY JUNIOR ledge (95 ft.).

FA Jessie Guthrie, Joey Murray 1975

If you miss any of the early microwire placements, this pitch will take on an **R** protection rating.

205 **THE BURN** 5.8 **PG**★

Just at the top of the wooden steps there is a big block with a small tree growing behind it. Start on the block, at a right-facing flake.

#1 Climb the flake or cracks in the face and continue up to a sloping ledge beneath an overhang and small right-facing corner. The belay at the top of the first pitch of ECSTASY will be to your right. (This route was originally done as two pitches, with the belay here.) Climb through the overhang and step left to a small stance. Climb the finger cracks straight up to the large ECSTASY JUNIOR belay ledge (100 ft.).

#2 Climb the center of the face to the right of the large corner (50 ft.).

FA Jeff Burns, Rich Pleiss 1974

The upper part of the first pitch has beautiful cracks on steep, clean rock. The second pitch is seldom done.

(Var.) The crux of THE BURN can be avoided by stepping left into a small right-facing corner with a tiny pine. This is known as BURN ESCAPE.

206 ALGAL FRIENDS AND FUNGUS 5.9 R

(Var.) Above the overhang midway up THE BURN, move right via the ramp and crack system to the southwest outside corner. Climb the outside corner to the large ledge.

FA Roman Dial, Mark Munn 1980

Lots of lichen and not much protection. Bring a #3 Friend.

207 TRAVERSE PITCH 5.5

(Var.) From a belay halfway up the BURN (or a short distance below the top of the first pitch of ECSTASY), traverse left and up onto the West Face to finish on the first pitch of ECSTASY JUNIOR. (50 ft.)

THE SOUTH END

The small stream that parallels Roy Gap Road flows through a dramatic gap south of the main summits. The truly imposing South End forms the north side of Roy Gap. The Southern Pillar lies on the south side of the gap and is described in the next chapter.

The formation is steep and complex, with several overhanging areas. Some of Seneca's most breathtaking routes ascend this wall, utilizing the many crack systems, corners, and three main buttresses.

Two or three pitches of climbing on the South End plus a little scrambling leads to routes as long as three more pitches on the upper South Peak. Despite the steep nature of the wall, several excellent moderate routes can be found here.

From left to right, major features of the South End are: Ecstasy Buttress, MUSCLE BEACH area, the Cave, Totem Buttress, another small cave area adjacent to the popular YE GODS, and finally the Skyline Buttress.

It can be difficult to retreat from the upper portions of routes that lie above the Cave if you are climbing with a single rope.

APPROACH
South End and Southwest Corner routes can be approached by the West Face Trail. The trail begins on the north side of Roy Gap Run, just west of the rock. Another option, especially when the stream is too high to cross, is to continue up the road and over a culvert pipe.

On the West Face Trail, hike 30 yards up the hill, until the trail cuts directly east to the Southwest Corner and the base of the Ecstasy Buttress. The rest of the South End routes can be approached by following the trail east along the base of the South End. The trail is marked with blue blazes.

Approach climbs on the far right side of the South End and the Southeast Corner by continuing on Roy Gap Road until about 50 feet past the culvert pipe. On your left, look for a post with a blue blaze. The trail climbs the talus only a few yards before turning left near the base of the Skyline Buttress.

PLEASE DO NOT forge your own way up through the fragile vegetation and talus directly below the South End.

DESCENT
All routes end near Luncheon Ledge on the West Face or Broadway Ledge on the East Face.

Routes climbing the entire South End finish either at a wooded area below Luncheon Ledge or on the southern tip of Lower Broadway Ledge. Walk and scramble following a blue-blazed trail back down to the base of the South End, or continue on to climbs on the upper crags.

There are also two rappelling options from the wooded area above ECSTASY and SIMPLE J. MALARKY. One involves finding the niche in the rock on the west side that takes you through to the top of ECSTASY JUNIOR. Make two 100' rappels from trees with fixed slings down this often crowded route.

The other option is a free-hanging double-rope (140') rappel from bolts near the top of SIMPLE J. MALARKY. The bolts are on a small ledge below steep slabs and should be approached on belay. An unroped slip here would result in a spectacular and certain death. This rappel deposits you on the talus just in front of The Cave.

208 **ECSTASY** 5.7 G★
Begin below the sloping buttress at the far left side of the South End.
#1 Climb 25 feet up the buttress, then continue through an easy chimney to a large ledge at the base of a white face with vertical cracks. Climb this face to a ledge beneath an overhang (100 ft.).

#2 Move right to a wide crack on the right side of the overhang. Climb up about 15 feet and then start traversing right and up across the wildly exposed face. Pass short cracks and move up to a small stance with several old fixed pitons (70 ft.).

#3 Make an easy 8-foot traverse right from the belay to the base of a steep crack. Climb up and over a bulge, then weave your way up until you can top out to the left of a pine that overhangs the face (55 ft.).

FA Joe Faint and party

This route is continuous and exposed, always exciting but never outrageous: a classic.

209 SOUTHWEST BUTTRESS VARIATION 5.5 G

(Var.) Climb the first pitch of ECSTASY. Begin the second pitch, but continue straight up the wide crack to a large ledge at the point where ECSTASY traverses right. Finish on ECSTASY JUNIOR or rappel 100 feet to the ground.

210 THE SHAMBLER 5.8

The start is the same as ECSTASY.

#1–3 Climb ECSTASY through its second pitch. Climb SJM ECSTASY CONNECTION.

#4 Traverse up and right, aiming for the bottomless black gully and a belay (50 ft.).

#5 Cross the gully and move across the Totem Buttress. Climb down to the TONY'S NIGHTMARE belay (60 ft.).

#6 Finish on TONY'S NIGHTMARE and SKYLINE TRAVERSE.

FA Ray Snead, Ben Mealy 1974

211 VALLEY VIEW 5.9 PG/R

Start on the right side of the large right-facing dihedral formed by the lower ECSTASY buttress. This corner is 15 feet right of the very toe of the Ecstasy Buttress.

#1 Climb the right side of the large dihedral, 5 feet right of the actual corner. Move through a small overhang with a prominent crack. This crack forms a right-facing corner. Continue to the top of the cracks. Climb diagonally up and left across the face, aiming for a shallow left-facing corner. Climb the corner, then head diagonally up and left to a belay on ECSTASY (140 ft.).

#2 Climb up and right to a small ledge. Climb up and left across the face. Follow discontinuous cracks to a small overhang. Move up and right, then back left, aiming for a small bush. From that bush, go straight up to the top (60 ft.).

FA Mike Perliss, Ed McCarthy

212 **SOUTHERN EXPOSURE** 5.9 **PG**

Start about 10 feet right of the start of VALLEY VIEW.

#1 Climb the broken face to a right-facing corner. Climb the corner. After about 40 feet the corner turns into a right-leaning ramp. This ramp leads to SIXTH SENSE. Instead of climbing the ramp, move left until it is possible to climb the left side of a small outside corner. Climb up past a small tree to the ECSTASY belay (150 ft.).

#2 Finish on ECSTASY.

FA Howard Doyle, Eric Janoscrat 1978

The protection is reasonable. Take many small to medium nuts and plenty of slings.

213 **SIXTH SENSE** 5.10a **PG**

Approximately 15 feet right of SOUTHERN EXPOSURE and 25 feet from the left side of the unmistakable Cave, there is a large, ugly corner. Start on the left wall on better-quality orange rock.

#1 Climb thin cracks and edges a short distance to the corner below the roof. Pull around the roof to the upper left-facing corner. Continue up, trending right to a good hanging belay with cold shuts (60 ft.).

#2 Continue up and left, passing several small overhangs. Climb past the traverse of ECSTASY and establish a belay at the base of the large right-facing corner at the top of the cliff (70 ft.).

#3 Climb the corner and the final overhang to the top (60 ft.).

FA Bob Williams, Barry Wallen 1966

FFA Matt Hale, Ray Snead 1973

214 MUSCLE BEACH 5.11a G★

Between the start of SIXTH SENSE and the left side of the large cave are several trees below a square cut roof.

#1 Climb up and left, aiming for a corner and crack on the left side of the large roof. Take the roof on the left and continue for about 15 feet to a hanging belay at cold shuts (50 ft.).

#2 Climb up and right to a niche. Continue up and over a bulge to a set of twin cracks. Climb the cracks until they end. Step left at the top of the cracks and climb steep rock to a cold shut belay at the far left side of the SIMPLE J. MALARKEY ledge (90 ft.).

#3 Climb the white corner for about 5 feet Step right, then continue straight through the roof (40 ft.).

FA Ray Snead, Matt Hale 1975

Take a trip to the BEACH this weekend, but don't get sand kicked in your face.

215 DRACULA 5.12a PG★

#1 Climb easy rock on the right side of a 20-foot tower just left of the Cave's mouth. Move left beneath the small roof. Move up and over the small roof, past three bolts. Traverse slightly left to MUSCLE BEACH to finish (a.k.a. DRACULA BEACH), or continue straight up past five or six more bolts to anchors at the lip of the SIMPLE J ramp.

FA Tom Cecil, Steve Cater 1989 (DRACULA BEACH, 5.11c)

FA Porter Jarrard 1991 (Direct Finish)

216 SUPERSTITION 5.11c PG/R

Start at the left edge of the Cave, at the same point as for DRACULA.

#1 Climb broken ledges 15 feet, to a large right-facing corner. Move up the corner for about 15–20 feet, until you reach the overhangs. Move left, then up through the large overhang to a hanging belay below the next roof (60 ft.).

#2 Turn the next overhang by moving left. Continue up a crack until it is possible to move right to a large right-facing open book. Climb the book to a corner. Climb the corner past a small tree to the SIMPLE J. MALARKEY ramp (70 ft.).

Harrison Shull on THE THREAT (5.12b). (Photo: Darell Hensley)

#3 Finish on SIMPLE J. MALARKEY.

FA Thayer Hughes, Mike Perraglio

FFA Eric Janoscrat, Howard Doyle 1978

This sustained route was free-climbed on Friday the 13th. Beware of bad rock on the second pitch. The route requires a large rack. Four-leaf clovers and rabbits' feet are optional.

217 SUPERSTITION DIRECT START 5.11d

(Var.) From the broken ledges at the start of the regular route, go up the left-facing corner, directly beneath the flared crack in the roof. Move through the roof and link up with the rest of SUPERSTITION.

FA Marty McLaughlin 1982

218 THE PROMISE A2

This aid route follows THE THREAT up to the fourth bolt, then moves left in a shallow arching corner past a fixed Bugaboo piton to cold shuts (80 ft.).

FA Harrison Shull 1999

Bring draws, hooks, nuts, brass, Lowe-balls, and cams up to 3 inches.

219 THE THREAT 5.12b G★

Begin just inside the Cave's mouth, right of a 20-foot pinnacle to the left of the Cave's mouth.

#1 Climb easy rock to a short flake and clip a bolt. Move up and slightly right on a steep, textured, orange face past more bolts, to a strenuous bulge with cracks on either side. Crank over this and climb on polished holds to a bolt anchor in an alcove. There are seven bolts in all (60 ft.).

FA Tom Cecil, Eric Anderson, Brian McCray 1992

220 FINE YOUNG CANNIBALS 5.12d/13a PG★

Begin inside the Cave, on the left (west) wall.

#1 Climb a shallow corner and a crack studded with old pitons, past three bolts. Clip the cold shut anchor but continue up and left, out and over the lip of the cave. Belay over the lip.

FFA John Bercaw, Rod Hansen 1988

This is the old SATISFACTION #1 aid route. The pitch was freed to the point of the cold shuts by Cal Swoager in 1981, creating Seneca's first 5.12 pitch (5.12c). An anchor nest of old slings and pitons at the top of this section was clipped as protection during the first ascent of CANNIBALS. In 1992 it was replaced by cold shuts and the three bolts were added.

221 THE PREDATOR 5.12a G
#1 Follow the line of four bolts to the right of CANNIBALS. Expect large air if you peel while trying to reach the fourth bolt.
FA Chris Tolen 1999
This short route is located entirely inside the cave.

222 CAVEMEN ?
Start near the back of the cave.
#1 Climb out the crack on the left side to the cold start belay on FINE YOUNG CANNIBALS.
FA Mark Carpenter, Barry Wallen
FFA Cal Swoager, Eric Janoscrat 1981
This is the old SATISFACTION #2 aid route. Look out for bats in the hand and finger locks. The traditional 5.10d rating seems improbable.

223 NIGHTMARE (project)
Start in the back right recess of the cave. A desperate line of upside-down climbing heads toward the lip of the Cave past several bolts.

224 SIMPLE J. MALARKEY 5.7 PG★
Start outside the right (east) side of the Cave entrance, just beyond a large ledge.
#1 Pick your way up the steep, black face directly below a large rubble-covered alcove. TCUs or similar thin cam protection make this a safer pitch (35 ft.).
#2 Ascend the obvious low-angle ramp that shoots up and left out of the alcove. The ramp is very narrow in one place. Continue past this break to the apparent end of the ramp (65 ft.).

#3 Climb up the steep wall and angle right to easier ground (60 ft.).
FA Jim McCarthy, Arnold Wexler 1954
FFA unknown
This is an interesting route through an overhanging wall, made possible by the large ramp that splits the face. Try one of the variations to finish. The best finish is perhaps the last pitch of MUSCLE BEACH (5.8), gained by continuing another 15 feet past the apparent end of the ramp (SJM WESTERLY EXTENSION).

A hair-raising incident occurred here in 1991: riled ground hornets stung a climber in the rubble-covered alcove at the top of the first pitch. The stung climber knocked rocks down toward the belayer and cut the rope. No one was seriously hurt—but you should watch for hornet holes under the debris! On another day a climber was just finishing the first pitch on a warm winter day when tons of ice suddenly crashed onto the ledge from high above, missing her by inches. These are only two of many known epics that seem to dog parties on this route. Most of the excitement seems to take place on the third pitch. Simple J. Malarkey was a *Pogo* cartoon strip character who parodied Senator Joseph McCarthy of 1950s Commie-baiting infamy.

225 SJM CAVE START 5.8 R
(Var.) At the right (east) side of the cave entrance is a short, smooth dihedral leading to overlapping roofs. This is only one of several ways to begin SJM from inside the Cave.
#1 Climb the dihedral past poor protection (or climb anywhere along the Cave wall farther left) and up the ramp to a point below the roof (good gear here). Clip nasty pitons over the lip and pull the roof. Work out right and up into the large rubble-covered alcove with a good-sized tree (55 ft.).
#2–3 Continue on SJM.

226 SJM WESTERLY EXTENSION
(Var.) At the end of the regular second pitch it is possible to move left around the corner another 15 feet to an exposed ledge at a right-facing corner. All variations to the last pitch (Routes 227–229) start here.

227 SJM TRAVERSE FINISH 5.6

(Var.) From the belay, climb straight up the corner about 10 ft until it is possible to traverse out right. Climb right, around the corner, to easier ground. Move up to the top (70 ft.).

228 SJM OVERHANG FINISH 5.8 ★

(Var.) This is also the last pitch of MUSCLE BEACH. Climb up the steep corner until below the obvious overhang. Pull the overhang at its widest point (40 ft.).

229 SJM ECSTASY CONNECTION 5.6

(Var.) It is possible to down-climb from the ledge and move left around a corner to the belay on ECSTASY. Finish by climbing the last pitch of ECSTASY.

230 WELCOME TO SENECA 5.10d R

The start is the same as SIMPLE J. MALARKEY.

#1 Climb the first pitch of SIMPLE J. MALARKEY.

#2 From the tree, climb the ramp to the right. Follow the ramp for 25 feet, to a white face. Climb the right-facing corner of the large flake, then move left. Continue straight up to the base of the flared chimney. Climb through the chimney and overhang to a small ledge (75 ft.).

#3 Climb the remainder of the buttress, keeping to the left side (100 ft.).

FA George Livingstone, Thais Weibel 1967

FFA Howard Doyle, Marty McLaughlin, Eric Janoscrat 1978

This strenuous route requires a large rack, but the crux is unprotected. There are areas of loose rock.

231 WILD MEN ONLY 5.11b PG

To the right of the Cave and SJM is the prominent sloping Totem Buttress, which rises to meet a large roof.

#1 Climb the buttress to a belay beneath the left side of the huge roof (90 ft.).

#2 Pull the overhang at its widest point, then continue up a squeeze chimney. After the chimney, continue to the base of an overhang. Traverse left, and then move up to a ledge (145 ft.).

#3 Stay to the right of the overhangs and continue up the buttress to the top (80 ft.).

FA Tom Evans, Chips Janger, Bob Lyon 1967

FFA John Bercaw, John Gorrahan 1976

232 TOTEM 5.11a PG★

Begin right of WILD MEN ONLY.

#1 Climb the Totem Buttress to a belay at cold shuts beneath the right side of the roof (5.5, 85 ft.).

#2 Follow the line of fixed pins out and over the roof (5.11). Belay at a small stance. Cold shuts (25 ft.).

#3 Follow the obvious inside corner up the buttress, through an overhang to a short wall. Climb the wall and move up to a stance. (125 ft.).

#4 Climb the corner to the top of the wall (50 ft.).

FA Ivan Jirak

FFA John Stannard 1971

233 SCROTUM 5.10a R/X

(Var.) Traverse about 10 feet, to the right of the roof pitch. Climb the overhang at this point (45 ft.).

This unprotected pitch takes balls to lead.

234 BLOOD ON THE TRACKS 5.10b R

Begin directly beneath the right side (east face) of the Totem Buttress, about 20 feet left of TONY'S NIGHTMARE.

#1 Climb the thin cracks in the center of the wall. Aficionados claim the left edge of the buttress is off route (70 ft.).

FA Leith Wain, Mark Huth

235 **THE GUMBY PATROL** 5.11b **PG**

Start at the top of the first pitch of TOTEM or TONY'S NIGHTMARE.
#1 From an ancient slung rock anchor, move up and slightly right to a bolt.
From there, move up into a thin left-facing corner. Climb to the roof, then
follow a line of five bolts up the face and eventually out onto the arête to
cold shuts (90 ft.).
FA Harrison Shull, Aaron Fullerton, Dave Cox
Bring a rack that includes HBs and RPs or the like.

236 **TONY'S NIGHTMARE** 5.6 **PG**

Start just to the right of the Totem Buttress below an obvious A-shaped
chimney. The route starts on the ramp below the chimney.
#1 Climb the ramp and corner to a sloping ledge at the base of a short wall.
Climb the wall and set up a belay beneath an overhang formed by a large
chockstone (70 ft.).
#2 Climb past the chockstone into the large chimney. Start up the chimney
until it is possible to exit right to a good ledge (50 ft.).
#3 Finish on SKYLINE TRAVERSE.
FA Tony Soler, Ray Moore, Lorraine Snyder 1950
The chimney is a favorite hangout for pigeons. The white stuff is not chalk.

237 **TONY'S NIGHTMARE DIRECT FINISH** 5.7

(Var.) On the last pitch, climb straight out the chimney and up the corner
above (95 ft.).

238 **EASY SKANKIN'** 5.9 **PG**★

#1 Climb past five bolts on the east-facing wall just left of TONY'S
NIGHTMARE DIRECT FINISH to a bolt anchor (50 ft.).

239 **QUARTZ INVERSION** 5.9 **PG**

Start high on the cliff, left of and slightly below the start of EASY
SKANKIN'.
#1 Climb discontinuous cracks in the wall to a tree at the top (75 ft.).
This climb is a good alternative finish for NIGHTWINGS.

240 **PYTHON** 5.9 **R**

Start above and to the right of the second pitch of SKYLINE TRAVERSE and about 30 feet right of TONY'S NIGHTMARE DIRECT FINISH.

#1 Climb the overhanging rock rib inside the east wall of the Skyline Chimney. Exit right about 4 feet from the top.

FA Paul Anikis, Howard Doyle

241 **BIRDS OF PREY** 5.10b **R**

Begin from the top of the second pitch of SKYLINE TRAVERSE.

#1 Climb the thin rounded flake in the center of the west-facing wall of the chimney right of PYTHON.

FA Howard Doyle, Mark Thesing 1984

242 **SPINNAKER** 5.11a **G**★

#1 Climb the outrageous face and overhanging arête right of BIRDS OF PREY. There are eight bolts and a cold-shut anchor at the top.

FA Darell Hensley, Chris Leon 1992

This route shares the same fin as LA BELLA VISTA. The climbs converge near the top.

243 **THE DAYDREAM** 5.9+ **R**

This route starts back down on the ground. Just to the left of the YE GODS corner, there is an obvious rectangular cave. Start near the left side of the cave.

#1 Climb the steep, grungy, loose and dangerous wall to a belay at the base of the large overhangs (70 ft.).

FA Howard Doyle, Lotus Steele 1975

244 **NIGHTWINGS** 5.10b

Climb THE DAYDREAM or TONY'S NIGHTMARE to the ledges at the base of the large overhangs to the left of YE GODS.

#1 Climb up the left-facing corner near the left side of the roof. Continue up overhanging corners to a small pedestal beneath the main roof. Climb through the roof, then step up to a belay. Strenuous and loose (85 ft.).

FA Chick Holtkamp, Carol Black 1978

Gina Hoag leading the superb YE GODS AND LITTLE FISHES (5.8).
(Photo: Bill Webster)

Warning! Helmets may not be protection enough for the next four routes if anyone is climbing SKYLINE TRAVERSE.

245 YE GODS AND LITTLE FISHES 5.8 G★

The large buttress on the right side of the South End (Skyline Buttress) forms a huge left-facing corner. Start at the ramp at the bottom of the corner and immediately right of the rectangular cave.

#1 Climb the steep corner straight up to a large ledge. Locate cold shuts high and to the right (85 ft.).

#2 Use the orange and black flake on the left wall in the back of the wide chimney to surmount the overhang. Finish on the second pitch of SKYLINE TRAVERSE (60 ft.).

#3 Finish on SKYLINE TRAVERSE.

FA Arnold Wexler, John Reed, Earl Mosburg 1953

FFA unknown

246 DROP ZONE 5.11b PG★

Begin to the right of YE GODS, on the right wall of the huge open book (west face of the Skyline Buttress).

#1 Climb horizontal and vertical cracks straight up the smooth, steep wall. There is one fixed pin. Cold shuts (85 ft.).

FA Marty McLaughlin, Howard Doyle, Eric Janoscrat 1978

Consider using double ropes. Alternate clipping may shorten falls.

247 CANDY CORNER 5.6 G★

Start at the base of the narrow left-leaning dihedral 15 feet to the right of DROP ZONE.

#1 Climb the dihedral to its top. Belay at cold shuts on the ledge above DROP ZONE and YE GODS or continue up and right to the SKYLINE TRAVERSE belay (95–110 ft.).

#2 Finish on SKYLINE TRAVERSE.

A fine route, steep yet moderate.

248 **LSD (LOWER SKYLINE DIRECT)** 5.5 **PG**

Begin in a gully on the lower section of the east side of the Skyline Buttress below and right of the start of CANDY CORNER.

#1 Climb up the broken section past a large tree until the climbing starts to get a little harder (80 ft.).

#2–3 Climb a narrow left-facing corner with fixed pitons until it's possible to stem right to the large flake on the first pitch of SKYLINE TRAVERSE. Finish up the first pitch of SKYLINE. It is also possible to stay low and right after the first pitch of LSD and traverse to the base of the regular first pitch of SKYLINE. Another variation moves left into the wide crack/narrow chimney on the left, which is followed to the ledge atop CANDY CORNER.

FA Paul Bradt, Don Hubbard, Sam Moore 1939

249 **SKYLAB** 5.9 **PG**

(Var.) Instead of climbing the entire second pitch of LSD, move to the crack in the center of the east face, between the variations described above. Climb it for 20 feet and move right in a 5.8 corner to rejoin SKYLINE.

FA Greg Collins, Paul Billups

250 **LA BELLA VISTA** 5.10a **PG**★

This route starts at about the same level as the top of the first pitch of LSD. It follows the edge of the thin fin formed by Skyline Buttress.

#1 Climb the right edge of the very narrow buttress, past an overhang, to the SKYLINE TRAVERSE belay ledge.

#2 From the rappel bolts at the start of SKYLINE TRAVERSE, climb up the steep arête, passing the final overhang on its left side (85 ft.).

FA Howard Doyle, Lotus Steele

This route shares the same fin as SPINNAKER. The routes converge near the top.

251 **LOTUS VARIATION**

(Var.) At the overhang on the first pitch, move right to a crack. Follow the crack to the top of the first pitch.

THE SOUTHERN PILLAR

From the Town of Seneca Rocks, the main bulk of Seneca's twin peaks are clearly visible to the left of Roy Gap. The Southern Pillar is a series of long narrow buttresses and chimneys that rise from the hillside on the right side of Roy Gap. There is a concentration of good climbs in an amphitheater formed by the west wall of the Pillar's main buttress and a north-facing wall marked by shallow caves. Other routes are located above and to the right of this central area, and on the east side of the Southern Pillar.

The GEPHART-DUFTY route and the top of the Pillar area have *lots* of loose rock, so be careful not to bomb those below. Natural rockfall has been observed coming from this area and is more likely during and after severe weather.

APPROACH

The hike to the Southern Pillar is the shortest approach at Seneca. Take the climbers' access trail beyond the Forest Service steel bridge, or the concrete low-water bridge at the new Discovery Center parking area, to Roy Gap Road. Walk up Roy Gap Road to a large boulder on the right side of the road. On this boulder is a memorial plaque to Sneza Kelly, who died in a fall at Seneca in 1982. Just past the boulder and before the Roy Gap Run culvert, a trail cuts up and right through rocks and hemlock roots.

GEPHART-DUFTY, RHODODENDRON CORNER, and SLIPSTREAM (routes 264–266) are reached first at the northwestern corner of the long western buttress system. Routes 268–297 are best approached by following the base of the amphitheater wall, beginning at SLIPSTREAM and heading up and right. Routes 252–263 are on the east side of the Southern Pillar. Routes are described left to right, starting with the uppermost route on the east side of the Pillar.

To approach the routes on the east face of the Pillar, it is necessary to hike up a steep, dirty and vegetated scree slope just east of the ramps at the base of Initiation Buttress without the benefit of a trail. This awful approach, which is never pleasant, is at its worst in the middle of summer.

DESCENT
The best descents, which allow you to avoid the steep, vegetated slope on the east side of the Southern Pillar, are by rappel. Climbs that have rappel anchors are so described. Rappel anchors can be found in the CLIMBIN' PUNISHMENT area, as described in the next section.

Climbin' Punishment Area: There are a number of anchors near the classic route CLIMBIN' PUNISHMENT.
- Find anchors at the top of the original third pitch. These cold shuts are less than 200 feet above the ground, but snags from retrieving a two-rope rappel are a definite possibility.
- Another set of cold shut anchors is 45 feet below, just right of ROY GAP CHIMNEYS, at a ledge with a square block under a smooth roof.
- Sixty feet lower still, on the west-facing wall, is a tree with slings. This anchor is 80 feet above the ground.
- Inside the chimney, 60 feet below the ledge with the square block and shuts, is another pair of cold shuts. These are about 70 feet above the ground.
- The anchors at the top of the third pitch of CLIMBIN' PUNISHMENT can also be reached if you top out on ROY GAP CHIMNEYS. Scramble carefully to the left.

Other Anchors: There are bolt anchors above SLIPSTREAM, RIGHT TOPE, BLOCK PARTY, BROWN BETTY, and UP YOURS. Because the cold shuts above DAYTRIPPER also serve SLIPSTREAM, they are located farther left than the end of the top of the original first pitch.

If you top out on some long routes in the central and east face areas, such as the fourth pitch of CLIMBIN' PUNISHMENT or GEPHART-DUFTY, descend by one rappel from a tree and then about a hundred yard of scrambling down the east side.

For the next five routes scramble about 100 yards up the loose, dirty, and trail-less east side of the Southern Pillar. At a point some 60 feet left of the edge of the upper Initiation Buttress; find a large, rough, orange-colored roof. THE FRAGMATIST begins on a narrow vegetated ledge at the left end of the roof.

252 **THE FRAGMATIST** 5.7
Begin on a narrow vegetated ledge below the left edge of the large overhang.
#1 Climb the crack to the left side of the left-facing corner to the ledge. Climb a 5.6 crack to the left of the corner to a large tree. Continue through an overhanging wall to a tree (115 ft.).
FA Eric Janoscrat, Pannil Jones 1983

253 **MYSTICAL MEMBRANE** 5.9
Start on the same ledge as THE FRAGMATIST.
#1 Climb the crack to the left-facing corner. Move onto the right wall and climb it to a tree (90 ft.).
#2 About 10 feet right of the tree is an alcove in an orange face. Climb the crack and left-facing corner straight to the tree (40 ft.).
FA Chris Guenther, Eric Janoscrat, Pannil Jones

254 **INTO THE MYSTIC** 5.7
Start several feet right of MYSTICAL MEMBRANE, near the left edge of the large overhang, just left of right-facing flakes and corners.
#1 Start below the roof, then move up and left. Work through on the left side, and then move up to the lichen-free area on the wall. Continue to easy ledges (65 ft.).
FA Harvey Graef, Bob Johnson 1977

255 AWAY FROM THE FLOW 5.9–

Start to the right of INTO THE MYSTIC. This route climbs over the center of the large orange roof.

#1 Climb up the right-facing flakes and corners directly to the large roof. Climb over the roof to a left-facing corner/detached pinnacle. Continue up the face, just left of the pinnacle. Move left 8 feet and continue up the crack system and face to the ledge.

FA Howard Doyle, Mike Whitman

256 SILENT SCREAM 5.9+

Start 8 feet right of AWAY FROM THE FLOW.

#1 Climb up and right, aiming for a large right-facing corner that splits the overhang near its right end. Surmount the small roof to gain the corner. Move up to the larger roof, then traverse left 10 feet to the nose. Climb over the nose and up the face to a tree near the right-hand side of the ledge.

FA Howard Doyle, Mike Whitman

257 A BITTER END 5.9+

About 45 feet down and right of the orange roof is a low, smooth wall with a thin crack. This is just a few yards left of the edge of the upper Initiation Buttress, and some 200 feet above the start of GEPHARDT-DUFTY.

#1 Climb the crack approximately 25 feet to the tree. Belay 15 feet left of the tree in the corner.

#2 Climb the crack in the center of the face to the overhang above. Traverse right for about 10 feet to the end of the overhang. Climb a right-facing corner to a belay (75 ft.).

FA Howard Doyle, Eric Janoscrat 1980

258 MRS. ROBINSON 5.6 ★

This climb follows the right-facing corner/flake system just left of the edge of the Initiation Buttress. This climb is located about 20 feet right of the start of A BITTER END, and several feet left of the arête of SOUTHERN THRILLER. Approach as for INITIATION, or climb the thin crack (5.7) used by those routes.

#1 Climb straight up the crack, aiming for a vegetated ledge (40 ft.).
#2 Climb the chimney (100 ft.).
#3 Move up and left to a large block. Climb to the top of the block, then left to a ledge (100 ft.).
FA Roger Birch, Bob Robinson 1970

259 SOUTHERN THRILLER 5.11b
Climb the first short crack pitch of A BITTER END. Move several feet right until a moderate crack can be seen heading up to a light-colored arête. Alternately, climb INITIATION to this point.
#1 Climb straight up the arête past six bolts to a cold shut anchor (50 ft.).
FA Tom Cecil, Darell Hensley 1993

260 INITIATION 5.6
This route is located on the eastern buttress. Start from a ledge on the buttress, just left of GREAT CHIMNEY.
#1 Climb the narrow north face to a ledge near the top (135 ft.).
#2 Finish easily up to the top.
FA John Markwell, John Christian 1971
This route is rarely done. Beware of loose rock.

261 GREAT CHIMNEY 5.1
Begin directly at the base of the large chimney that splits the main Southern Pillar into the GEPHART-DUFTY (west) and INITIATION (east) buttresses.
#1 Climb the chimney to a belay (150 ft.).
#2 Continue to the top (115 ft.).
FA Mark Carpenter, Tal Bielefeldt 1965

262 HIDDEN GEM 5.10
This route is found on the east face of the highest fin of GEPHART-DUFTY. Approach as for SOUTHERN THRILLER, or go up GREAT CHIMNEY to the base of the wall.
#1 Climb the right side of this face past four bolts and some protection placements to a bolt anchor (60 ft.).
FA Aaron Fullerton, Harrison Shull

263 **CRAVING FOR PINK** 5.7

#1 Climb the finger crack right of HIDDEN GEM to the same anchor.

FA Aaron Fullerton, Harrison Shull

264 **GEPHARDT-DUFTY** 5.7 **PG**★

This route climbs the longest buttress system of the Southern Pillar. The line follows the narrow, stepped, north-facing wall of the first (western) buttress reached by the short trail from Roy Gap Road.

#1 Climb the narrow wall either on dark, blocky rock to the left (5.5) or via a crack system near the right edge (5.8). Climb gradually easier terrain to a large sloping ledge. Build your own anchor below and left of the SLIPSTREAM cold shuts. (90 ft.).

#2 Continue to the base of the tower (75 ft.).

#3 Climb to the top of the tower (25 ft.).

#4 Cross the notch and climb the north face of the buttress (60 ft.).

#5 Traverse across the top of the GREAT CHIMNEY to the neighboring buttress. Climb it to the top (60 ft.).

FA Bob Gephardt, Bob Dufty

This route offers spectacular situations, although on sometimes questionable rock. Route finding is difficult in places. Many variations are possible.

265 **RHODODENDRON CORNER** 5.7

Start at the base of the GEPHART-DUFTY buttress.

#1 Climb the 5.7+ /5.8– version on the right side of the north face of the buttress (as for G-D var. mentioned above). Move up to SLIPSTREAM shuts (90 ft.).

#2–3 Climb the easier but badly vegetated corner system to the right. This crack runs diagonally across the west face of the G-D Buttress to the top (150 ft.).

FA John Christian, Arnold Wexler

266 SLIPSTREAM 5.10a PG★

The start is 25 feet right of the west buttress arête, where left-trending ledges allow access to the nice wall to the left.

#1 Climb up flakes several feet to the ledge. Traverse left for 10 feet, then climb the lower of the two left-trending flake systems toward thin cracks, then a left-facing corner/flake. Follow the flake to a sloping ledge and scramble 15 feet to cold shuts (75 ft.).

FA Howard Doyle, Chris Rowins

267 SLIPSTREAM DIRECT 5.10a

(Var.) This variation appears to take the higher line of left-trending flakes and holds to the thin cracks and corner/flake.

FA Howard Doyle, Eric Janoscrat

268 STOP MAKING SENSE 5.12b R

Located just right of SLIPSTREAM.

#1 Climb the face just right of the regular start of SLIPSTREAM. Climb a crack to a horizontal crack. Continue past a bolt to the top of SLIPSTREAM (75 ft.).

FA Greg Smith, Mike Artz

269 DAYTRIPPER 5.10a G★

Begin as for SLIPSTREAM.

#1 Climb up and right into the narrow right-leaning, right-facing corner that starts 20 feet off the ground. Follow the corner to its end. Traverse up and left toward the buttress and look for cold shuts above SLIPSTREAM (80 ft.).

#2 You can climb easier rock to the top, although most parties do only the first pitch.

FA John Bercaw, J. Garrahan

270 **DOUBLE D DIRECT** 5.11c **PG**

(Var.) From a hanging belay at the end of the first pitch of DAYTRIPPER, traverse left to an obvious vertical crack. Climb the thin cracks and face to a stubby evergreen tree and ledge (50 ft.).

FA Drew Bedford, Ed Begoon, Mike Artz 1986

The protection is good but difficult to place.

271 **DAYTRIPPER DIRECT** 5.11a **PG**★

#1 Set up a hanging belay at the end of the right-facing corner of DAYTRIPPER (60 ft.).

#2 Climb the crack for 10 feet, until you reach a horizontal crack. Traverse right along the horizontal crack to another vertical crack. Climb this crack to a ledge (100 ft.).

Up the grade if you do it in one long pitch. The protection is good but difficult to place.

272 **SWEET RELEASE** 5.12a **R**

Start 15 feet right of the DAYTRIPPER start, just left of a large rectangular block with a hand crack on its west face. Move up a narrow left-facing corner. Angle up and left to a sloping ledge and clip a rusty old bolt (as of this writing). Go up to a crack, then finish on DAYTRIPPER DIRECT.

FA Mike Artz, Eddie Begoon

273 **RIGHT TOPE** 5.9 **G**★

Begin left of CLIMBIN' PUNISHMENT below a small inside corner. This is just left of the main dihedral containing the starts to CLIMBIN' PUNISHMENT and ROY GAP CHIMNEYS. Start by climbing onto the large rectangular block.

#1 Climb the crack and left-facing corner about 40 feet to a small overhang. Move past the overhang by climbing the face on the right side of the crack. Continue up the flake and stem and lie-back on the left. Belay at cold shuts (95 ft.).

#2–3 Climb easier rock to the top.

FA Herb Laeger, Eve Uiga

274 TIGHT ROPE 5.9

(Var.) Instead of climbing the undercling/lie-back crux of RIGHT TOPE, follow a flake up and right, to a thin crack and face with a bolt. Belay at a tree (100 ft.).

FA Darrell Hensley, Sandy Fleming, Dave McCutcheon 1993

275 CLIMBIN' PUNISHMENT 5.9+ **PG★**

Begin below and just left of the obvious ROY GAP CHIMNEYS at a dihedral with a ramp at its base, a smooth left wall, and a nice continuous corner crack.

#1 Climb the dihedral for about 45 feet, to a small ledge on the left. (This is an optional belay if desired.) Continue up the beautiful corner past small overhangs to a lower-angled ramp (5.7–5.8, 120 ft.). Beware: the anchors just below the orange roof are poor, and there is a huge loose block.

#2 Climb to the roof in the dihedral and pass it on the left. Continue up the corner to cold shut anchors on the left wall (70 ft.).

#3 After a short scramble left across a vegetated ledge, climb a short, clean crack on the west face (40 ft.).

FA Herb Laeger, Mike Goff, John Markwell

Many parties avoid the last pitch (5.9+), which is good PG climbing, although a little off the line. This is a vertical crack in the west-facing wall above a vegetated area. The first two or three pitches make an excellent 5.8 route.

276 ROY GAP CHIMNEYS 5.6 **PG★**

Start as for CLIMBIN' PUNISHMENT.

#1 Start up the ramp and corner crack, but move right and tackle the squeeze chimney, passing a small tree. Move up into the obvious wider chimney. Continue to a belay at cold shuts on the left wall (80 ft.).

#2 Continue up the chimney to a good ledge on the right, with cold shuts. Most people descend from here (80 ft.).

#3 Continue up the chimney, then move right onto the buttress. Climb up a short corner to the top (40 ft.).

FA Tom McCrum, Roger Birch April 1969

Beware of loose rock at the top.

277 DISCO DEATH MARCH 5.10b G★

Start about 8 feet right of ROY GAP CHIMNEYS.

#1 Move up the narrow north-facing wall, just right of a small roof that is 10 feet above the ground. Pass thin cracks and face holds up to a vertical crack located a few feet right of the small ROY GAP CHIMNEYS tree. Continue up the crack and move left into ROY GAP CHIMNEYS after about 70 feet of total climbing.

FA Howard Doyle, Eric Janoscrat

A strenuous route with good protection.

278 D.D.M. DIRECT FINISH 5.10d R

(Var.) Instead of moving left to the chimney, continue straight up the north face of the buttress/arête.

FA Ed Begoon, Howard Clark 1989

Bring small TCUs and other thin gear.

279 JUDGE NOT 5.9

Start just around the corner from DISCO DEATH MARCH.

#1 Climb the face just left of the blocky orange section to the sloping ledge (40 ft.).

#2 Continue up the face using the leftmost crack system. Move left past a bolt to the left corner of the face. Pass the JUDGMENT SEAT alcove and move up and right onto the upper face. Follow a thin vertical crack left of JUDGMENT SEAT to the large ledge (50 ft.).

FA Sean Cleary, Ashton Walton, John Wright 1989

280 THE JUDGMENT SEAT 5.10a G/PG★

Start in the slot cave where the west face of the Pillar meets the more rotten north-facing wall of the amphitheater.

#1 Bridge the first few feet of the cave until it is possible to move up and left. Follow an undercling flake to a severely sloping ledge. Continue up a steep wall with some iffy rock, to a triangular alcove. Climb out the alcove and up a steep off-fingers crack to a large ledge (70 ft.).

#2 Move right and follow cracks until below a large smooth roof. Step right and continue up to the top (145 ft.).

FA Jeff Burns, Bill Webster 1975

281 **ELECTRIC CHAIR** 5.9

Start at the obvious slot cave.

#1 Climb the right side of the slot cave until it's possible to reach a flake on the left. Continue up the arête and discontinuous crack system on the left to a small hardwood tree with rappel slings. There are three bolts (70 ft.).

FA Ed Begoon, Darell Hensley 1986

282 **BIZARRE GRANDIOSE** 5.9

Use the same start as ELECTRIC CHAIR.

#1 Climb the right side of the cave until it is possible to reach a flake on the left wall. Climb the flake, then go straight up the corner to a ledge (100 ft.).

FA Greg Collum, Ron Augustino 1975

A 5.8 variation can be climbed a few feet right of the normal crux.

283 **POINT MAN** 5.11b

Start at the obvious slot cave.

#1 Climb up the right side of the slot cave to the roof. Follow the crack through the roof and belay at the tree (35 ft.).

FA Howard Doyle, Marty McLaughlin, Eric Janoscrat 1981

284 **AMBUSH** 5.11a **G**★

Begin in the center of the blocky overhanging wall right of the slot cave. There may be flycatcher nests on the wall.

#1 Climb the overhanging orange wall via good holds. Continue up a short hand crack and some painful fingerlocks. After a few more moves, gain a ledge with a tree and cold shuts. This anchor is shared by BLOCK PARTY, AMBUSH's neighbor to the right (40 ft.).

FA Howard Doyle, Eric Janoscrat, Marty McLaughlin 1979

This good climb does have some loose rock.

285 **BLOCK PARTY** 5.8 **PG**★

Start a few feet right of AMBUSH below a left-facing corner system.

#1 Climb the left-facing corners to a ledge with cold shuts (45 ft.).

#2 Go up and left past blocky grunge to a platform.

FA Matt Hale, Ray Snead 1975

Watch for loose rock. Most parties avoid the second pitch.

286 MENTAL BLOCK 5.10b/c

This new line is really a direct finish to BLOCK PARTY. Stand below BLOCK PARTY and locate an overhanging white/gray arête 30 feet above the anchors at the end of the first pitch.

#1 Climb the first pitch of BLOCK PARTY to the anchors. Keep going up and across fairly loose but very easy terrain until below the roof/arête. Pull the roof onto the right side of arête to find incut jugs. Climb up the right side of the arête and protect with nuts. Pass one bolt to a two-bolt anchor (80 ft.).

FA Harrison Shull, Paul Fomalont 1998

Don't follow the loose and vegetated corner left of the arête.

287 BORDER PATROL 5.11c **X**

Start up on the ledge a couple of feet right of BLOCK PARTY.

#1 Boulder up and right on light gray rock, past an ominous chunky flake and small left-facing corners, to a ledge.

FA Rob Robinson, Robyn Erbesfield 1984

This route was altered in 1989 after local climber Mike Artz broke several holds and fell. He avoided injury on this dangerous route by placing gear in the adjacent BLOCK PARTY. The climb is not known to have had an ascent since this mishap.

288 BROWN BETTY 5.12d

This is the leftmost of two bolted climbs that exit the rotten cave just right of BLOCK PARTY and AMBUSH.

#1 Climb up and out of the deepest part of the cave, trending left. This route joins UP YOURS near the top. There are five bolts if you use the first and last bolts of UP YOURS (45 ft.).

FA Brian McCray 1993

289 UP YOURS 5.12a

Start in the right margin of the cave.

#1 Climb out of the shallow cave on blocky holds to better rock, then up the overhanging face to cold shuts. There are six bolts (45 ft.).

FA Brian McCray 1993

290 APPENDICITIS 5.7

Start about 15 feet right of UP YOURS and 40 feet left of the west edge of the wall.

#1 Climb the wall up and under the dihedral. Head left until it is possible to climb the wall to the left of the dihedral (110 ft.).

FA Eric Janoscrat, Len Sistek 1976

291 THE LEMUR 5.5

Near the right (west) side of the rotten wall mentioned above is a corner. Begin 30 feet left of the corner.

#1 Climb the vegetated face and angle left to a slightly overhanging wall. Belay at a large pine on the tree-covered platform. Descend by rappelling (65 ft.).

FA Eric Janoscrat, Len Sistek 1976

The following five routes are on a separate buttress above and to the right of the previous routes.

292 FEAR OF FLYING 5.8 ★

Hike around the right end of the rotten wall of the LEMUR. Go upslope about 80 feet. This climb follows the first crack system left of the outside corner of the buttress.

#1 Climb the chimney and right-facing corner to the overhang. Move left and up, then step back right into the crack system. Climb the cracks to the top (100 ft.).

FA Rich Pleiss, Gene Genay 1975

293 THE VICTIM 5.7

Start just left of the dihedral mentioned in FEAR OF FLYING.

#1 Climb the face and crack, aiming for a squeeze chimney. Climb through the chimney and head straight to the top (100 ft.).

FA Rich Pleiss, Gene Genay 1975

294 EXIT FROM THE VICTIM 5.4

(Var.) Climb the normal route until it is possible to step left 5 feet to an easy corner. Follow the corner to the top. This variation avoids some bushwhacking at the top.

295 ROLLING ROCK 5.8

Scramble past the starts of FEAR OF FLYING and the VICTIM to the base of the smooth west-facing slab high on the cliff.

#1 Climb the loose wall to the right of the slab, aiming for a left-leaning groove. Climb left under the groove, then up the face to easier rock. Continue up a left-leaning cleft through the overhang. Climb this cleft to the top (120 ft.).

FA Eric Janoscrat, Jim McAtee 1978

Take plenty of small wires for the climb and fortitude for the approach.

296 STONEYS 5.7

The start is the same as ROLLING ROCK.

#1 Climb the slab to its end (70 ft.).

#2 Ascend the right wall to a corner. Follow the corner to a roof. Surmount the roof using cracks. Once above the roof, climb the thin crack that splits the face (120 ft.).

FA Eric Janoscrat, Jim McAtee 1978

297 QUIT DOGGIN' THE SCENE 5.8+

This route starts down and left of the smooth ramp and climbs steep rock on a separate formation above the BLOCK PARTY area.

#1 Scramble to a sloping ledge below a large overhang. Climb the overhang to cracks in the center of the face. Continue up these to the top.

FA Greg Collins, George Flam 1981

SOUTH PEAK–EAST FACE

The East Face of the South Peak contains some of the most gorgeous stretches of rock at Seneca. The routes above Upper Broadway, especially from DINAH MOE HUM to GUNSIGHT TO SOUTH PEAK DIRECT, are among the very best in the valley. Here you'll find long (200+ ft.)., continuous moderate routes like CONN'S EAST and excellent shorter face and crack climbs from 5.7 to 5.12. The face is especially attractive during the cooler months, when the east-facing rock bakes in the morning and early afternoon sun.

The South Peak–East Face can be separated into three distinct areas:

Southeast Corner: A triangular area that lies below Broadway Ledge and marks the north edge of Roy Gap. See the photos on pages 164 and 166.

Lower Broadway Ledge Area: An area of rock that extends from the east side of the Humphrey's Head to the Upper Broadway Chimney. See the photos on pages 169 and 175.

Main East Face: The steep wall that rises from Upper Broadway Ledge. See the photos on pages 179, 187, and 188.

APPROACHES
Southeast Corner. Walk east 50 feet past the culvert carrying Roy Gap Run under Roy Gap Road and find a blue-blazed trail on the left. (Please do not hike up the fragile scree slope above the culvert pipe.) This trail forks almost immediately, with the right branch leading up to the area at the base of SKYLINE TRAVERSE and WORRELL'S THICKET and the left branch traversing west across the base of the South End. A spur to the Scramble Trail (see below) is also found on the way up to the Southeast Corner.

Lower Broadway. Do a climb on the Southeast Corner or South End or go around the end of the crag from the west as follows: Hike up the West Face

Climber on the Upper Broadway Chimney. It's easy but a fall would be fatal.

Trail to Luncheon Ledge, at the base of Humphrey's Head. Walk south from Luncheon Ledge and down-climb to the left (east) to the south end of Lower Broadway. Once you're on the southern end of Broadway Ledge, you can access the central and far right (Upper Broadway) Chimneys areas of the East Face by scrambling north. 4th class terrain is encountered at the Lower and Upper Broadway Chimneys.

Upper Broadway Ledge. From Roy Gap hike the East Face climbers' trail known as the Scramble Trail (a.k.a. Cardiac Hill). Follow Roy Gap Road for about 80–100 feet, past the culvert pipe in the Gap, and find a blue blaze and signpost at a small cut in the road bank on the left. Walk up and right and find the rest of the Scramble Trail as it follows a low rocky ridge to a point even with the Gunsight Notch. Take a feeder trail (blue arrow and blazes) left (west) to 3rd class and 4th class ledges. After an initial 10-foot rock step, scramble left and up about 60 vertical feet to Upper Broadway Ledge. The "path" from the end of the feeder trail to Broadway Ledge follows 3rd class and 4th class ledges and steep, must-not-fall terrain and arrives at the base of CASTOR and POLLUX, both distinctive thin 5.10 cracks in pale rock. These climbs are about 60 feet from the North end of Broadway Ledge and the Gunsight Notch.

It is also possible to access Upper Broadway from the Gunsight Notch. Reverse EAST FACE TO GUNSIGHT NOTCH (5.0).

DESCENTS
From the Summit Ledge
Near the end of the last pitch of OLD LADIES', it is possible to rappel from a large tree with slings and rings. From this tree you descend 75 feet to fixed anchors at the top of the first pitch of FROSTED FLAKE. From there it is 60 feet to the Broadway Ledge. Two ropes will place you directly on Broadway Ledge in one rappel. (Warning: The trees on the traditional OLD LADIES' Rappel Route, which descends the East Face from the southernmost point on the Summit Ledge, are no longer safe.)

From the Summit

There are three rappel anchors on the South Summit proper, all for East Face rappels. One is down in a small keyhole notch about midway along the exposed crest of the Summit Ridge, roughly above GREEN WALL as seen from the west and above ALCOA PRESENTS on the East Face. There are two more east-face bolt anchors on a ledge 8 feet up and left of the anchor in the little notch. It is 165 feet to Broadway from the keyhole notch. You need 200-foot ropes to get down from the anchors up and left. Sixty feet directly below the keyhole notch, there are two more pairs of fixed rappel anchors on the Alcoa Ledge. From there it is 100 feet to Broadway Ledge; 65 feet lower is another pair of anchors halfway up the first pitch of CONN'S EAST DIRECT (about 40 ft. above the ledge).

From Upper Broadway Ledge

To reach the East Face Trail on foot from Upper Broadway, locate the initial 4th class down-climb near the base of CASTOR and POLLUX. Follow narrow ledges to the north and down, until you reach the trail. It is possible to rappel down the West Face after doing South Peak–East Face climbs by climbing (5.1) into the Gunsight Notch from the north end of Upper Broadway. See page 71.

SOUTHEAST CORNER

The Southeast Corner rises in a gigantic triangle, extending north from the edge of the South End. All of the routes on the Southeast Corner end on the southern part of Lower Broadway Ledge.

298 SKYLINE TRAVERSE 5.3 G★

The climb begins on a large ledge with a detached chimney/flake that forms a right-facing corner. This is about 25 feet to the right of the outside (south) edge of the Southeast Corner. First climb a short wall (5.1) to the wide ledge with trees. Some parties prefer to use a dirty crack to directly gain the chimney/flake.

#1 Climb up the crack and face that are right of the chimney/flake to a good ledge. Climb the left-facing corner 10–15 feet to a horizontal crack. Move left a few feet to an airy ledge at the intersection of the South End and the East Face. Two bolt anchors facilitate descent from this point (90 ft.).

#2 Step off the belay ledge and make very exposed moves to the left in order to reach a wide chimney. Climb the wide chimney, then continue up to a low-angled area. There is much loose rock (70 ft.).

#3 Continue up the chimney to its end at the south end of Broadway Ledge. Avoid the loose gully at the top of the pitch by stepping right early to solid rock and a trail (50 ft.).

FA Paul Bradt, Don Hubbard, Sam Moore 1939

This is one of the finest routes of its grade. The start of the second pitch has filled the hearts of many beginning climbers with fear. The position is airy, but the protection is excellent. USE CAUTION: There is a large amount of loose rock at the top of the climb, and some of Seneca's most popular routes are directly below you. In fact, it is unwise to be at the base of YE GODS, DROP ZONE, and CANDY CORNER without a helmet.

299 OLD TIMER'S LUCK 5.8

Start at the beginning of the second pitch of SKYLINE TRAVERSE. This route goes up between PYTHON and BIRDS of PREY.

#1 Continue up the corner crack on the right side of the chimney. Climb the steepening crack to the top of the South End.

FA Don McIntyre, Dan Kearney 1993

300 REAR ENTRY 5.8+ PG ★

From the two-bolt station atop the first pitch of SKYLINE.

#1 Climb right and up past gear placements and six bolts. Gain and pull the left side of the large DUFTY'S POPOFF roof and continue to the top of the buttress (125 ft.).

FA Harrison Shull, Di Botello 1999

Bring pro to 3 ½ inches.

301 **HERO PENDULUM** 5.5 **R**

Start at the end of the first pitch of SKYLINE TRAVERSE.

#1 From the belay ledge, move right around the large block to a horizontal line of weakness. Follow this to WORRELL'S THICKET (110 ft.).

FA David Kepler, George Pinkham

302 **CAPTAIN TRIVIA** 5.8 **R**

Begin 15 feet to the left of the DUFTY'S POPOFF corner beneath a broken overhang.

#1 Leave the SKYLINE TRAVERSE belay ledge and move right until below the overhang. Climb the face and pass through the overhang on its left side. Continue up the face and merge with DUFTY'S at the roof. Finish on the normal route (130 ft.).

FA Leith Wain, Matt Lavender 1978

The protection is poor at the crux.

303 **DUFTY'S POPOFF** 5.7 **PG** ★

Start 20 feet to the right of the end of the first pitch of SKYLINE TRAVERSE, past a large block.

#1 Move right to the base of the prominent left-facing inside corner. Climb the corner, past orange-colored rock, to an overhang. Move over the roof and climb the face above and left to the top (130 ft.).

FA Art Gran, Bob Dufty 1959

A nice climb with an exciting crux. The easy (5.4 or 5.5) face above the roof has almost no protection.

304 **DUFTY'S POPOFF DIRECT** 5.9 **R**

(Var.) Begin below and right of the normal start and climb a crack to a tree. Move left to join with DUFTY'S POPOFF.

FA Cal Swoager, Greg Phillips 1980

305 **KAUFFMAN-CARDON** 5.4

Use the same start as DUFTY'S POPOFF.

#1 Move right from the belay until at the DUFTY'S POPOFF corner. Climb the right wall of the corner then traverse up and right across the buttress to easier climbing. Continue to a tree (100 ft.).

#2 Traverse right on a ledge to a left-facing corner system; follow this until it is possible to move up to Lower Broadway Ledge (75 ft.).

FA Andy Kauffman, Betty Kauffman, Joan Ascher, Phil Cardon 1954

306 **BEE STING CORNER** 5.7 **G**★

(Var.) At the end of the first pitch of KAUFFMAN-CARDON, it is possible to climb a large left-facing corner (50 ft.).

FA George Livingstone, Arnold Wexler, Andy Kauffman

307 **CARDON'S RIB** 5.4 **R**

(Var.) From the end of the first pitch of KAUFFMAN-CARDON, step right and then climb straight up the arête and east face to the right of the BEE STING CORNER (50 ft.).

FA Phil Cardon, John Christian 1970

308 **THE TOMATO THAT ATE CLEVELAND** 5.9

Begin on the same ledge as the start to SKYLINE TRAVERSE, a few feet to the right of the chimney.

#1 Climb the thin right-trending cracks to a larger crack and a tree. Move past this tree to the start of the DUFTY'S POPOFF corner (45 ft.).

#2 Climb DUFTY'S POPOFF.

#3 Walk left to the steep arête overhanging the ledge. Climb the arête (40 ft.).

FA A. Clarke, D. Kepler, D. Mong 1973

309 **H&H** 5.7 **R**

Begin right of the tree ledge where SKYLINE starts and left of the vegetated ramp that is WORRELL'S THICKET.

#1 Climb the broken face, aiming for the prominent corner of BEE STING. About midheight of the first pitch, climb just to the right of a prominent roof. Belay at the base of BEE STING CORNER (100 ft.).

#2 Move left on the ledge until it is possible to climb the face above. Move through a small overhang, step left, and climb the face above (60 ft.).
FA Herb Laeger, Howard Doyle
The route is poorly protected. A better-protected variation of the first pitch goes through the overhang.

310 WORRELL'S THICKET 5.0
About 150 feet uphill (north) of the edge of the Southeast Corner is a long, vegetated, low-angled ramp.
#1–2 Climb the right-leaning ramp in two easy pitches, until Lower Broadway Ledge is reached at a point below UP AND COMING (200 ft.).
FA Ed Worrell, Blondie Worrell

LOWER BROADWAY LEDGE
The Broadway Ledge extends the full length of the South Peak–East Face. The Lower Broadway Ledge is the section from the south end near Humphrey's Head to the Upper Broadway Chimney. Routes near the south end lie above the Southeast Corner and below and to the left of Humphrey's Head.

HIGH TECH and WIND UP start about 80 feet left of the top of WORRELL'S THICKET at the first significant outcrop at the south end of the Broadway Ledge. This formation is exceedingly loose on top.

311 HIGH TECH 5.9 PG
Start left of Humphrey's Head at an orange face.
#1 Climb the ramp up and right. Continue up the thin crack that angles left to the top (50 ft.).
FA Parker Hill, Hernando Vera 1981
There is also a 5.10 top-rope direct start.

312 WIND UP 5.5
Begin at the right-facing corner/flake at the right side of the outcrop.
#1 Climb up and right to a ledge. Follow the left crack to the top (70 ft.).
FA Jessie Guthrie, Tom Whitesol 1974

313 **REVERSE C** 5.1

From the south end of Broadway Ledge, walk to a point about 20 feet from the left side of the east face of Humphrey's Head, just right of the start of WIND UP. Begin below a shallow rotten flake.

#1 Climb the huge left-facing, C-shaped flake up to the top of the small formation below and left of Humphrey's Head.

#2 Continue up the south ridge of Humphrey's Head.

FA Bob Gephardt, Cliff Alexander 1957

314 **A CHRISTIAN DELIGHT** 5.4 **G**★

Begin directly below Humphrey's Head, where the wall is recessed.

#1 Move up easy tree ledges to a clean, steep corner facing left. Climb this and a small overhang. Step into a small alcove and move up, passing bushes and some loose rock (80 ft.).

#2 Move up and to the right. Climb up to the notch between the Cockscomb and Humphrey's Head (60 ft.).

FA John Christian and party 1970

This route may be done as a single 140-foot pitch.

315 **MIDWAY** 5.7

Start a few feet right of A CHRISTIAN DELIGHT.

#1 Climb straight up to a small pine growing out of a steep wall just below a left-facing flake about 25 feet up from the starting ledge. Climb up on the left side of the tree and straight up to a large ledge. Step right and climb 12 feet, to another ledge (70 ft.).

#2 Step right to a sloping corner facing right and climb up and slightly left to the base of Humphrey's Head. (Var.: A 5.8 finger crack can also be used here.) Head up Humphrey's to a crack with several old pitons (70 ft.).

FA Pete Grant, John Christian 1983

COCKSCOMB

WINDY
NOTCH

HUMPHREYS HEAD   18

313

314

324

314   316

329

328

LOWER BROADWAY LEDGE

316 UP AND COMING 5.4 G★

Begin below and even with the right edge of Humphrey's Head. This start is right of the recessed area where A CHRISTIAN DELIGHT begins.

#1 Move up easy ledges to a left-facing inside corner. Stem up and then trend slightly right. Aim for the large ledge at the base of the south face of the Cockscomb (165 ft.).

FA June Lehman, John Christian, Sally Greenwood 1970

The route can easily be broken into two pitches if you want.

Routes 317–320 are located on the East Face of the Cockscomb and all start on the easy traverse ledge of the second pitch of OLD LADIES'. See photo on page 171 and the description of OLD LADIES' on page 88. OLD LADIES' starts on the West Face but soon passes through a notch onto the East Face at the intersection of Humphrey's Head and the Cockscomb.

317 DIANE 5.9 R

Begin approximately 10 feet to the left of I.O.W. below a small overhang. This is just right of the end of the first pitch of OLD LADIES'.

#1 Climb through the overhang to a flaky, brown face. Step left to a narrow, severely overhanging arête. Continue up the arête to a shallow chimney. Follow the crack to the top (90 ft.).

FA Chris Kulczycki, Steve Schneider, Chris Rowins 1979

Seldom if ever done. There is much loose rock.

318 INCREDIBLE OVERHANGING WALL 5.11a R

Begin about 10 feet to the right of the start of the second pitch of OLD LADIES', below a thin arching crack.

#1 Climb the face and arching crack up the overhanging wall to a no-hands rest. From there move right 10 feet, then up the lichen-covered wall to the top (90 ft.).

FA Greg Hand, Mel Banks 1976

319 **GIBBS EXCELLENT** ?

Begin about 3 feet to the left of the pine tree growing in the center of the second pitch of OLD LADIES'.

#1 Climb the face over the bulge to a fixed pin. Continue up the face (90 ft.).

FA Chris Rowins, Steve Schneider 1979

Seldom if ever done.

320 **COCKJOB** 5.7

Begin just to the right of GIBBS EXCELLENT and almost directly behind the small tree that grows only inches from the rock.

#1 Climb the face and thin crack up and right until it merges with DISCONTENT. Finish on DISCONTENT (80 ft.).

FA Chris Rowins, Chris Kulczycki, Steve Schneider 1979

Seldom if ever done.

321 **WINDY CORNER** 5.4 **G**★

Begin from the large pine at the end of the second pitch of OLD LADIES'. You can also start to the left at the big hardwood near the base of the crack.

#1 Climb the crack that leads up to the Windy Corner notch that separates the Cockscomb from the main South Peak. From the blocky ledge in Windy Notch climb the large corner over a chockstone and on up to the Summit Ledge (80 ft.).

322 **JANE'S ROUTE** 5.2

Use the same start as WINDY CORNER. The JANE'S ROUTE flake is to the right of the Cockscomb, on the east face of the South Peak proper.

#1 Climb inside the large, grungy left-facing corner/flake that lies just to the right of WINDY CORNER and just left of the OLD LADIES' chimney/rib. Scramble up loose terrain to the Summit Ledge (50 ft.).

FA Jane Showacre

323 **AMAZING GRACE** 5.7 **R**

Start at the end of the second pitch of OLD LADIES'. This route is not on the Cockscomb.

#1 Traverse straight out right from the belay on easy ledges to a tree (35 ft.).

#2 Climb to about 15 feet from the top of the second pitch of DIRTY OLD MAN (60 ft.).

#3 Traverse up and right across the East Face until it is possible to drop down on top of the Soler Flake (120 ft.).

FA Larry Conrad, Mike Schmitt 1974

This route has several long runouts.

Routes 324–327 start on the right end of Lower Broadway Ledge, between Lower Broadway Chimney and Upper Broadway Chimney.

324 **LADY ELAINE** 5.5 **PG**

Begin just above the short chimney that breaks the Broadway Ledge (Lower Broadway Chimney). This is about 30 feet right of UP AND COMING.

#1 Climb the face up and right in order to reach a crack. Follow the crack for about 30 feet, until it is possible to traverse to the right across a lichen-covered face. Aim for a ledge with a small pine tree. From the ledge, move left on small ledges to easier ground. Climb up to the exposed belay at the top of the first pitch of OLD LADIES' (120 ft.).

FA Mark Thorne, Ray Friend, Earl Devault

325 **ANGEL'S WING** 5.9– **X**

Begin about 15 feet right of LADY ELAINE.

#1 Climb straight up from the bottom to a stance 10 feet left of the first bolt on HIGHWAY TO HELL. Trend up and left.

FA Cal Swoager, Eric Janoscrat, Terry Ivanhoe

No protection worth speaking of. Take hooks.

326 **HIGHWAY TO HELL** 5.10a **R**★
Start 15 feet left of the Upper Broadway Chimney.

#1 Climb the scruffy face to a small, rotten overhang. Move past the overhang to the much finer face above. Ascend the face past two bolts to easier ground (80 ft.).

FA Eric Janoscrat, Cal Swoager

Some protection can be placed at the horizontal break below the sparsely bolted face.

327 **EXPLETIVE DELETED** 5.7
Start below the Upper Broadway Chimney, right of HIGHWAY TO HELL. Begin from the top of a mound of debris.

#1 Climb the wide crack to a ledge. Move up and left to intersect with OLD LADIES' near the right side of the Cockscomb. Traverse right and belay beneath the DISCONTENT crack (85 ft.).

#2 Climb DISCONTENT for a few feet, until it is possible to move right to a small orange crack. Follow this flake and crack up and right. Easier ground leads to the summit of the Cockscomb (90 ft.).

FA Dan Taylor, Todd Eastman 1974

UPPER BROADWAY LEDGE
The Broadway Ledge extends the full length of the South Peak–East Face. The Upper Broadway Ledge is the section from the top of the Upper Broadway Chimney to the ledge's end at the Gunsight Notch. Starting with DISCONTENT, most of the following climbs start on the Upper Broadway Ledge.

328 **DISCONTENT** 5.6 **R**
Start from the top of Upper Broadway Chimney. Begin just left of an obvious curving flake.

#1 Climb the broken face and crack to the left of the flake. Belay on the ledge that runs beneath the Cockscomb. This ledge is also the second pitch of OLD LADIES' (35 ft.).

#2 Climb the face aiming for an obvious orange crack. Climb the crack and face to the top of the Cockscomb (85 ft.).
FA Rich Pleiss, Bill Webster 1974

329 DINAH MOE HUM 5.9+ PG ★

Start below a left-facing corner with a thin crack and short arête at the right edge of a very smooth face.
#1 Climb the face and thin cracks on the outer edge. Move right from the corner (crux) to an easier face. Climb large holds up to the tree at the end of the last pitch of OLD LADIES' (45 ft.).
FA Jessie Guthrie 1975

330 RAPPEL DOWNS HORSERACE 5.7 R

This route climbs the system of flakes and cracks 15 feet right of DINAH MOE HUM. These lead to a sparse pine and the ledge directly below Windy Notch. This is also the start of the last pitch of OLD LADIES'.
#1 Climb the flakes that angle slightly left. Pull the small overhang and climb straight up to the rappel tree.
FA Eric Janoscrat, Cal Swoager, Howard Doyle 1981

331 DEEP THROAT SUNDAY 5.9- R

Start between RAPPEL DOWNS HORSERACE and the prominent left-facing flake of DIRTY OLD MAN.
#1 Climb right-facing flakes for 20 feet, then move right for about 7 feet onto a lichen-covered face. Climb straight up.
FA Eric Janoscrat, Cal Swoager

332 RASP 5.8

Start about 10 feet left of the DIRTY OLD MAN corner/flake.
#1 Climb the face to the top.
FA Howard Doyle, Paul Anikis, Eric Janoscrat
Long after the first ascent, four bolts were added by a party that was unaware the route already existed. Once little done, this route is now popular; as of this writing, though, better anchors are needed to handle the heightened level of traffic.

Chris Lea on MR JONES (5.11 b/c). (Photo: Bill Webster)

333 **DIRTY OLD MAN** 5.6 **PG** ★

Begin beneath an obvious left-facing corner/flake that lies approximately 10 feet off of the ground and about 40 feet to the right of Upper Broadway Chimney. This is the left side of the exfoliating plate that also forms FROSTED FLAKE on the right.

#1 Climb the short wall to a small ledge beneath the corner/flake. Follow the corner/flake up, and then move 20 feet right to a good belay at bolts (80 ft.).

#2 Move left and climb toward a steep, narrow right-facing corner. Climb the corner to the Summit Ledge. Beware of loose rock at the top of this pitch (75 ft.).

FA Charlie Fowler, Jon Harris, Dave Bushman 1973

334 **ICING ON THE CAKE** 5.11d **PG**

Begin a few feet right of DIRTY OLD MAN and 30 feet left of FROSTED FLAKE.

#1 Climb the wall past two bolts to a ledge (50 ft.).

FA Pete Absolon 1988

335 **PUT A WIGGLE IN YOUR STRIDE** 5.11d **R**

Start just left of the base of the obvious, thin, right-facing FROSTED FLAKE.

#1 Climb the super-crimpy face past four bolts (50 ft.).

FA Eddie Begoon, Daniel Miller 1988

336 **FROSTED FLAKE** 5.9– **PG** ★

Start about 30 feet right of DIRTY OLD MAN at a thin right-facing flake. The flake arches up and right and ends in a small overhang.

#1 Climb the crack to the overhang at its end. Move over the bulge, then back left to a small belay ledge and cold shuts (50 ft.).

#2 Climb up and right to a chunky left-facing corner. Climb the corner for about 10 feet, then move left onto the face. Climb over a series of bulges to the top. This pitch is comparatively poor in quality (75 ft.).

FA Jim Callahan, Linda Connelly, Brock Baker 1974

337 **KID GALAHAD 5.9** PG

#1 Climb the first pitch of FROSTED FLAKE. Climb straight up the orange face past a bolt to good holds.

FA Gary Hahn, Chris Rice, Josh Rice

Protection is somewhat sparse.

338 **T. R. RAP AND TAP** 5.11d

Start about 20 feet right of FROSTED FLAKE at a block leaning against the wall.

#1 Climb through an orange streak in the smooth wall and continue up past a small right-facing corner. Six bolts to cold shuts.

FA Mike Perliss 1985

This old death-route was retro-bolted in 1994.

339 **MISTER JONES** 5.11b/c **PG★**

Start on the large sloping ledge about 30 feet left of the obvious left-facing corner of SOLER.

#1 Climb the face past seven bolts to shuts (80 ft.).

FA Eddie Begoon, Mike Artz 1988

Very sustained.

340 **BROTHERS IN ARMS** 5.12b **R**

Start several feet left of SOLER on a sloping ledge.

#1 Climb the face past seven bolts to a small roof. Climb the roof to a flake. Finish at a small pine.

FA John Bercaw, John McGowan 1988

The R protection rating is due to the distance to the first bolt. Bring a #4 Friend or similar piece.

341 **HIDDEN ASSETS 5.10c PG**

Start as for SOLER.

#1 Climb SOLER for 20 feet, through the vertical wide crack. Move left on jugs past at least one nut placement, to a line of six well-spaced bolts.

FA Art Brown, Harrison Shull 1998

A 60-meter rope and small nuts are needed.

342 **SOLER** 5.7 **PG** ★

Begin at the obvious, quite large, left-facing corner that starts on a ledge 10 feet up. This corner curves right to the true summit of the South Peak. The corner is formed by the immense Soler Flake.

#1 Climb the wide crack and steep corner until it curves right and forms a ledge. Belay at a narrow ramp leading up and right, or move 15 feet farther right on the ledge to cold shuts (135 ft.). Stemming and offwidth moves in the first 30 feet take you past places where a 7- or 8-inch piece or two would make this pitch a good bit safer.

#2 Climb the narrow ramp and diagonal break that leads to a small left-facing corner in the steep wall above. (Committing 5.7 face climbing leads up to the aforementioned corner if you belay from the shuts to the right of the original second-pitch start.) Climb through steep terrain, following good cracks. At the point where the crack system suddenly ends, climb up and left on face holds to a small ledge and easier terrain, which appears just when it's needed. Follow the crack up and right to the very summit of the South Peak (110 ft.).

FA Tony Soler, Ray Moore 1951

The second pitch is spectacular, a great achievement for 1951.

343 **SOLER ESCAPE** 5.6 **PG**

(Var.) Near the end of the first pitch of SOLER, climb out and left to the base of a grungy-looking orange crack. Climb the crack past the overhang to a tree. Climb past the tree to the Summit Ledge (75 ft.).

344 **TALBERT PICKLEFISH** 5.9- **R**

Begin at the end of the first pitch of SOLER.

#1 Down-climb the flake until it is possible to traverse out left to the obvious crack about 8 feet away. Follow the crack straight up and finish between two trees (90 ft.).

FA Dennis Grabnegger, Dick Miller 1973

345 **PICKLERIGHT** 5.9

(Var.) Climb the TALBERT PICKLEFISH crack until it is possible to move to the right. Move up to the Summit Ledge (120 ft.).

FA Jeff Burns, Randy Gainer 1973

346 **NATURAL MYSTIC** 5.10d **PG**

Start at the cold shuts located just right of the top of the first pitch of SOLER.
#1 Make committing moves to a bolt, then climb over a slight bulge past two more bolts and gear placements. Cold shuts (80 ft.).
FA Tom Cecil, Tony Barnes

347 **TERMINAL VELOCITY** 5.10b **R**

Start on Broadway Ledge approximately 10 feet right of the SOLER flake and about 6 feet left of the CONN'S EAST corner beneath a small left-facing corner.
#1 Climb the face past the left-facing corner and up incipient cracks for about 25 feet, to a horizontal crack. Move right and up. Use a small flake to access small lichen-covered cracks. Follow the cracks up to and over a bulge. Continue up to a belay (75 ft.).
#2 Finish on any other route that continues from the SOLER/CONN'S EAST flake.
FA Howard Doyle, Marty McLaughlin, Eric Janoscrat 1979

348 **TERMINAL ATROCITY** 5.10c **X**

(Var.) A direct start to TERMINAL VELOCITY. Climb the face just right of TERMINAL VELOCITY. On the first ascent, protection was placed from CONN'S EAST.
FA Pete Absolon, John Govi 1985

349 **TIME FLIES** 5.11a **PG**

The start is the same as CONN'S EAST.
#1 Climb the first few feet of CONN'S EAST, then move up and right over the moderate face to a bolt. Climb the face past two more bolts and thin protection placements to the top of the SOLER flake.
FA Howard Clark, Mike Artz, Eddie Begoon
Take RPs or HBs and #0 TCUs.

350 **CONN'S EAST** 5.6 **PG**★

Start at the prominent left-facing corner system, 20–30 feet right of SOLER. There is a pile of blocks at the base, above a short rise in the ledge. This corner is formed by the Conn's East Flake, which eventually merges with the Soler Flake.

#1 Climb the leftmost short corner up and right to a chockstone in the main Conn's East Flake. Pull over this and continue up the huge flake. It's possible to get off route on an excellent, steep 5.7 lie-back variation to the left. The regular route goes right past ledges and a small tree to the chimney behind the flake. Go up this route, then traverse right along the top of the flake until easy progress is barred by a small corner/flake and slightly overhanging wall. Cold shuts (5.5, 130 ft.). Some parties belay below the chimney to avoid rope drag.

#2 From the end of the ledge move up the flake a short distance and out right onto the steep, exposed face. Move up and right over a bulge, past a fixed pin, to welcome buckets. Traverse right 20 feet, to a bolt anchor on the Alcoa Ledge, a long ledge below ORANGEAID and ALCOA PRESENTS (5.6, 50 ft.).

#3 Move to the right end of the ledge to an arching left-facing crack formed by a large flake. Climb the flake to the base of a chimney. Move past the large chockstone into an easy gully and up to a large ledge (70 ft.).

#4 Climb the north edge of the South Summit crest and walk the ridge south to the summit blocks (100 ft.).

FA John Stearns, George Kolbucher, Bob Hecker, Jim Crooks 1944

A classic. One of the best. The original second pitch went down the ramp to the ledge atop what are now CASTOR and POLLUX and re-ascended the short, steep corner that is now called CONN'S EAST DIRECT.

351 HOPEFUL ILLUSIONS 5.10d PG

Begin 20 feet right of the start of CONN'S EAST.

#1 Climb the face toward thin, sharp cracks and a very small right-facing corner. Above the corner, climb the face via shallow cracks. At this point the bolts on CHANGELING are about 10–12 feet to the right. From the end of the cracks, move up and left to a small bush, then move up to CONN'S EAST (75 ft.).

#2 Finish on CONN'S EAST.

FA Howard Doyle, Eric Janoscrat 1979

352 HOPEFUL ILLUSIONS DIRECT FINISH 5.11d R

(Var.) When the cracks end, continue straight up to a flake at the extreme righthand side of the small overhang. Then continue straight up to the top of the CONN'S EAST flake.

FA Kris Kline 1983

353 THE CHANGELING 5.11c PG★

Start approximately 30 feet to the right of CONN'S EAST. The right-facing TERRA FIRMA corner is to your right.

#1 Climb to the shallow, right-leaning flake and follow it about 25 feet to its end. Move up past two bolts and a crack to the roof. Traverse left around the roof and up to a belay on CONN'S EAST (90 ft.).

#2 Finish on CONN'S EAST.

FA Jack Beatty, Jim Woodruff 1979

RPs or similar small protection are useful below the first bolt.

354 CHANGELING DIRECT FINISH 5.11b R

(Var.) Finish through the roof, using the shallow right-facing corner on the right.

FA Greg Smith 1985

355 TERRA FIRMA HOMESICK BLUES 5.11c PG★

Begin just left of the two thin cracks of CASTOR and POLLUX at a short but obvious right-facing corner.

*Bill Webster at the crux of THE CHANGLING
(5.11 b/c). (Photo: Kevin O'Brien)*

#1 Climb the corner to its end, then step left to a crack. Follow the crack until you are forced into thin face moves. Crank the crux and continue up to a horn. Continue up the crack to cold shuts (95 ft.).
FA Herb Laeger, Eve Uiga 1975
Small wired stoppers and TCUs protect this excellent route. There is a long runout above the crux.

356 **CASTOR** 5.10a **PG** ★

Several feet right of the TERRA FIRMA corner and approximately 50 feet north of the CONN'S EAST flake, there are two cracks splitting the wall. CASTOR is the left crack.
#1 Climb the thin face and crack system to a belay on a large sloping ledge (5.10, 45 ft.).
#2 Climb the ramp to cold shuts at the end of the first pitch of CONN'S EAST. These first two pitches are easily combined (5.4, 40 ft.).
#3 Climb straight up from the belay, starting in a juggy crack and moving up to chickenheads and a small roof. The 5.9– crux of this pitch is somewhat sparsely protected (90 ft.).
FA Pat Milligan, George Livingstone 1971
Most people climb only the first pitch, although the whole route is good. The 5.10 climbing on the first pitch ends after 15 feet, and the only tricky protection is also right off the ground. A tall person can get a piece in from high on the ledge.

357 **CASTOR TO TERROR** 5.11 **PG**

(Var.) Climb CASTOR for 30 feet, until you can angle up and left toward the large crack at the top of TERRA FIRMA. Finish on TERRA FIRMA.
FA Kris Kline
Not much new rock, but still an interesting route.

Scott Gilliam leading the thin crack of POLLUX (5.10a). (Photo: Bill Webster)

358 **POLLUX** 5.10a **G**★

Start at the right crack.

#1 Climb the crack to the large ledge (45 ft.). Bolts are located to the right on CONN'S EAST DIRECT.

#2 Rappel off or follow another route to the top.

The corner at the right end of the ledge is on CONN'S EAST DIRECT. The ramp and corner on the left are on CASTOR.

FA Pat Milligan, George Livingstone 1971

359 **ORION'S BELT** 5.11d/.12a

Start at the left side of the sloping ledge at the top of the first pitch of CASTOR and POLLUX.

#1 From the curving corner crack, step right and climb a narrow left-facing corner, protecting as well as possible. Climb the sphincter-clenching face above past three bolts. Move up and right past a seam to the CONN'S EAST/ALCOA belay ledge.

FA Ed Begoon, Howard Clark 1990

360 **CONN'S EAST DIRECT START** 5.8 **PG/R**

Begin 10 feet right of POLLUX, beneath a crack system with an initial blank section and diamond-shaped block 10 feet above the ground. Above the block is an obvious shallow chimney.

#1 Climb the sequential, unprotected face to the block. Above the block, climb the crack and chimney to a good ledge with a bolt anchor. Continue up the crack and left-facing corner to a ramp. Ascend the ramp up and well to the right until it's easy to get on the right end of the Alcoa Ledge (two bolted rap/belay anchors) (100 ft.).

#2 Finish on pitches #3 and #4 of CONN'S EAST, or do ALCOA or ORANGEAID.

FA Arnold Wexler 1954

361 **TRIPE FACE BOOGIE** 5.9+

(Var.) Climb CONN'S EAST DIRECT START for about 15 feet Step left to a crack. Climb the crack to the first good ledge. Finish on the normal route.

FA Dieter Klose, Savvy Sanders 1977

362 **BOGTROTTER** 5.9 **R**

(Var.) Start from the good ledge with a bolt anchor about 40 feet up CONN'S EAST DIRECT. Climb the narrow corner and face straight up aiming for the Alcoa Ledge (45 ft.).

There are only two or three micronuts for protection on the upper face.

FA Marty McLaughlin, Mike Endicott 1977

Routes 363–367 start on the Alcoa Ledge, 90 feet above Upper Broadway Ledge. The ledge is accessed via CONN'S EAST, CONN'S EAST DIRECT, ORION'S BELT, and BOGTROTTER.

363 **GRAND FINALE** 5.9+ **PG**★

Start from the left end of the Alcoa Ledge.

#1 Traverse 10 feet left of the prominent ORANGEAID finger crack, along the easy ledge. Climb up along the shallow right-facing corner, then up the face trending a little left to the summit (70 ft.).

FA Eve Uiga, Herb Laeger

364 **ORANGEAID** 5.10b **G**★

Start just left of the leftmost bolt anchor on the Alcoa Ledge.

#1 Climb the orange cracks up to the roof. Surmount the roof (it's easier on the right), then move up easier rock to the summit (80 ft.).

FA Mark Carpenter, Barry Wallen 1966

FFA John Stannard 1971

365 **GATORADE** A2–A3

A route up the very thin seams between ORANGEAID and ALCOA was led by Greg Smith.

366 **ALCOA PRESENTS** 5.8+ **G**★

Begin several feet right of ORANGEAID.

#1 Climb the cracks just left of the right-hand bolt anchor to a narrow overhang. Climb the shallow right-facing corner and face above to a notch in the summit ridge (65 ft.).

FA Joe Faint, Mike Nicholson
FFA Tom Evans, Bob Lyon, Bob Williams 1968
An enjoyable route that tempts many into standing on a pin. As you pass, note the solid, over-driven, aluminum piton after which the route is named.

367 THE VISION 5.6
Begin on the same ledge as ORANGEAID and ALCOA.
#1 Climb the face several feet to the right of ALCOA. Aim for orange-colored rock. Climb the orange rock up and to the left, aiming for the summit (95 ft.).
FA D. Klose, N. Maynard
Instead of moving left, it is also possible to climb a 5.7 crack to the right.

Routes 368–377 start from Broadway Ledge right of CONN'S EAST DIRECT START.

368 VIETNAM VETERANS AGAINST THE WALL 5.11b R
Start on Broadway Ledge. Begin from a small block located about 10 feet right of CONN'S EAST DIRECT START.
#1 Climb the face up and right, aiming for a small yellow area of blocky rock. Continue up and left and follow shallow cracks until they end. When slightly above a bush on the left, traverse left to a crack system. Move up the crack and merge with CONN'S EAST DIRECT (65 ft.).
FA Marty McLaughlin, Cal Swoager 1981

369 SPOCK'S BRAIN 5.11a G ★
Start just to the right of V.V.A.W. at a right-facing corner.
#1 Climb the corner and move slightly right into thin cracks. Follow the crack system up to a narrow left-trending flake. Follow the flake and narrow corners up and left to the CONN'S EAST DIRECT flake/ledge, just below the north end of the Alcoa Ledge (100 ft.).
FA Leith Wain, Jack Beatty 1979
Climbing directly up to the cold shuts is a little harder. Take small wired nuts and TCUs.

370 **HIGH TEST** 5.9+ **PG**★

Begin several feet right of SPOCK'S BRAIN below a sickle-shaped ledge.

#1 Climb up past a smallish right-facing flake, a few feet right of the small right-facing corner that marks the start of SPOCK'S BRAIN. Continue up shallow cracks and knobs to the sickle-shaped ledge (25 ft.).

#2 Move up the narrowing, left-facing corner at the right end of the ledge. Climb the thin corner until it is possible to move right to shallow cracks. Climb the cracks to face moves below an overhang and right-facing corner. Climb the steep right-facing corner to a good stance. Follow cracks and flakes to the top. Bolts with rap rings (120 ft.).

FA Herb Laeger, Eve Uiga 1974

An excellent route that offers much variety. Double ropes or lots of long slings are useful if you aim to do it in one pitch. For the descent, a single 60-meter rope will just reach the top of the block at the start of NIP AND TUCK.

371 **HEAVY FUEL** 5.12c **PG**

Use the same start as HIGH TEST.

#1 Climb the first 20 feet of HIGH TEST and step left on the narrow sickle-shaped ledge. Climb up past four bolts to the ledge where SPOCK'S BRAIN ends.

FA Ed Begoon, Darell Hensley, Tom Cecil

372 **UNLEADED** 5.9+ **PG**

Use the same start as HIGH TEST.

#1 Climb the first 80 feet of HIGH TEST to the right-facing corner. Traverse left 15 feet, to a ledge.

#2 Step back onto the face and climb straight up, then slightly right to a left-facing flake. Climb slightly left via a thin crack. Use the same anchor as for HIGH TEST.

FA Hunt Prothro, Howard Doyle

This route can be done as a single pitch.

373 NITRO 5.10d R

Begin about 7 feet right of HIGH TEST. Climb the thin seam that is not quite a crack to the sickle-shaped ledge.

FA Cal Swoager, Mike Artz 1983

The protection is thin.

374 LOW OCTANE 5.11b PG ★

Climb a shallow crack system just to the right of NITRO. This merges with HIGH TEST at the traverse past the sickle-shaped ledge.

FA John Bercaw, Jim Nigro

375 TICKET TO RIDE 5.10c PG

Use the same start as LOW OCTANE.

#1 Climb flakes just right of LOW OCTANE. Move right to gain a crack. Follow the crack through an 8-inch overhang and climb up to intersect with NIP AND TUCK. At the crux of NIP AND TUCK, step left to an undercling at a roof. Pull through the roof into a lichen-covered crack. Climb cracks to the ledge below the summit. Belay at the bolts above HIGH TEST (135 ft.).

FA Mike Artz, Eddie Begoon 1983

376 NIP AND TUCK 5.10c PG ★

Begin from the right end of the large block at the extreme north end of Upper Broadway Ledge.

#1 Climb thin cracks up and left. Follow the crack system through the overhang and on up to the top (120 ft.).

FA Herb Laeger, Eve Uiga 1974

FFA Bob Richardson, Rich Perch, Herb Laeger 1974

377 EAST FACE TO GUNSIGHT NOTCH 5.0

Begin at the extreme north end of the Broadway Ledge.

#1 Climb up and right over easy left-facing flakes and corners close against the East Face. Continue into the Gunsight Notch (45 ft.).

378 GUNSIGHT NOTCH EAST 5.5 G

This route does not start from the Broadway Ledge. Begin from ledges directly below the Gunsight Notch that are attained by scrambling from the ground. The wide cracks to the left of this line are not as good.

#1 Climb directly to the notch, passing a few very old pitons (60 ft.).

FA Paul Bradt, Sam Moore, Don Hubbard

The next three routes climb a wall below Upper Broadway Ledge, directly below the start to SOLER.

379 PRAYING TO THE ALIENS 5.8 R

Begin 75 feet left of LUNGE OR PLUNGE, just 5 feet right of an easy scramble.

#1 Climb a shallow left-facing corner/flake to the ledge.

FA Mark Thesing, Ed McCarthy 1983

380 LUNGE OR PLUNGE 5.11d PG

Locate an orange-and-white wall directly below the start of SOLER.

#1 Climb the left-facing corner and the face above. Move past a bolt to the Broadway Ledge (60 ft.).

FA Howard Doyle, Eric Janoscrat

Cal Swoager was the lunger and plunger.

381 DC 5.9 X

This route also starts below the Broadway Ledge, just right of LUNGE OR PLUNGE.

#1 Climb a nice 5.8 crack studded with old army pins to a ledge.

#2 Move up and right past horizontals. Run it out to the Broadway Ledge.

FA Pete Absolon, M. Armbrecht 1988

NORTH PEAK–EAST FACE

The North Peak–East Face is not particularly striking when compared to other walls at Seneca. It's a low, somewhat broken face with little visual appeal that lies high on the hill. However, it contains several excellent routes and on crowded days may be the best area to visit if you wish to escape the throngs draped over the South Peak.

APPROACH
There are three approaches to the face.

Seneca Rocks Hiking Trail to the North Peak: Some parties walk up the Seneca Rocks Hiking Trail to the top, at the north end of the rocks. From here locate the top of the climbers' trail at the base of the East Face near ISADORA'S RUN and follow it down.

Scramble Trail (East Face Trail): Another good approach is to hike up the Scramble Trail (East Face Trail), which climbs the slope on the east side of the rocks. Hike through Roy Gap and continue up the road about 80 feet. Locate a blue-blazed trail on the left and follow it to a small rocky ridge parallel to the East Face. Hike steeply about 300 yards to a point about even with the Gunsight Notch. A spur trail turns toward the rocks and ends below the initial 3rd class terrain. By scrambling and walking up and right (north), you'll soon reach the area at the base of LICHEN OR LEAVE IT, etc.

From the South Peak: It is possible to reach the North Peak–East Face from the South Peak. From Broadway Ledge, scramble down exposed 3rd and 4th class rock to the ground. Continue over to the base of the North Peak.

DESCENTS
Getting off the North Peak summit ridge is an exposed scramble to the north with loose rock. Because of this, and because the second pitches of many North Peak–East Face routes are short and obscure, many climbs are usually done in a single pitch. Fixed anchors vary widely in type and quality; some routes have none.

382 GUNSIGHT TO NORTH PEAK 5.0

This is a long route that can be split into as many pitches as one desires. It starts in the obvious, wide chimney at the northeast corner of the Gunsight Notch.

#1 Climb to a ledge, then follow it to an inside corner.

#2 Ascend the corner to the top of the ridge.

#3–4 Follow the ridge to a chimney, then continue to the summit (300+ ft.).

FA Chuck Sproull, Sally Jordan, Peter Gardiner 1969

Use extreme caution. The summit ridge is tremendously exposed and has much loose rock.

383 EEYORE'S TAIL 5.5 PG

Start below the right edge of the Gunsight Notch.

#1 Climb up and right on easy ledges to an inside corner with a wide left-facing crack. Climb the corner up to an intersection with GUNSIGHT TO NORTH PEAK. This route lies just to the left of a smooth wall with the obvious zigzag cracks of LICHEN OR LEAVE IT (95 ft.).

FA John Christian, June Lehman 1971

Protection is adequate with large gear.

384 AS YOU LIKEN IT 5.10c R

Start 20 feet right of the EEYORE'S TAIL corner and about the same distance left of the more prominent thin, clean cracks of LICHEN OR LEAVE IT. Begin at a prominent clean streak with a finger and hand crack.

#1 Climb the face to a small overhang. Move through the overhang and up to the tree (50 ft.).

#2 Climb the face behind the tree for 30 feet, to a small overhang. Traverse right along the roof to the belay tree and rappel bolts on LICHEN OR LEAVE IT (50 ft.).

FA Howard Doyle, Eric Janoscrat, Cal Swoager

385 A.Y.L.I. DIRECT FINISH 5.10d R

(Var.) At the undercling, move straight up the white streak past two bolts.

FA John Govi, Eddie Begoon 1988

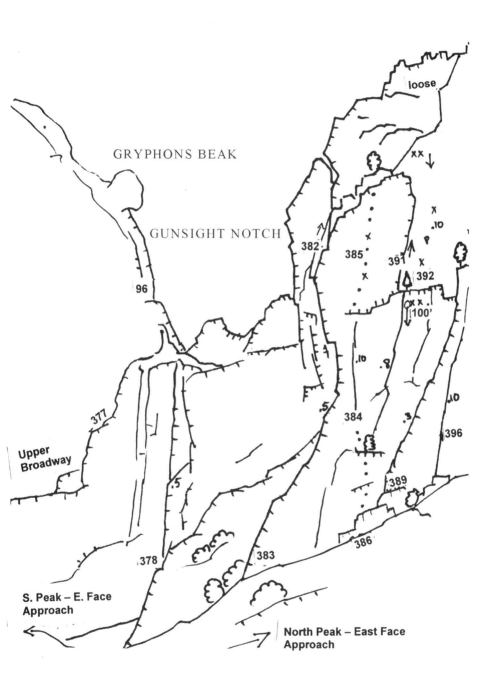

GRYPHONS BEAK

GUNSIGHT NOTCH

loose

386 **LICHEN OR LEAVE IT** 5.8 **PG**★

Start at the base of the smooth wall and thin cracks 30–40 feet right of EEYORE'S and 10 feet left of the large ROUX corner. You will have to scramble to a ledge about 10 feet up.

#1 Scramble to the large ledge. Climb up and left over 20 feet of moderate but runout (5.5 R) rock. From the tree mentioned on the previous route, climb right-trending thin cracks to a large tree ledge. Bolt rappel anchor (100 ft.).

FA Howard Doyle, Lotus Steele 1976

Take a number. Aesthetic cracks and good friction for the smeary footwork make this a favorite.

387 **HELTER SKELTER** 5.10c **PG**★

Use the same start as ROUX.

#1 Climb the ROUX corner until you're about 10 feet below the tree. Traverse left across the face to a thin crack in the face. Climb the crack to the large tree (100 ft.).

FA Howard Doyle, Lotus Steele 1976

Take thin crack pro including micronuts. The direct start (5.10 R/X) has been led but is usually top-roped.

388 **KEDS** 5.7

Use the same start as ROUX.

#1 Climb ROUX to the traverse that leads to HELTER SKELTER. Move left 3 feet and climb the larger crack up to the ledges (100 ft.).

FA John Gathright, Istvan Sugar 1986

389 **ROUX** 5.3 **PG**★

This follows the large left-facing corner to the right of LICHEN OR LEAVE IT and HELTER SKELTER.

#1 Climb the corner, mainly using the wall on the right, to a large pine tree on the conspicuous ledge (90 ft.).

#2 Follow easy rock up and right in a rubbly gully to the summit (60 ft.).

FA Maitland Sharpe, Linda Harris 1971

Routes 390–395 are located on the wall above LICHEN OR LEAVE IT, ROUX, and FINGER STINGER.

390 **LICHEN OR NOT** 5.11b **PG**

#1 Climb the face and thin cracks to the right of A.Y.L.I. DIRECT. May be done as a direct finish to LICHEN OR LEAVE IT.

FA Harrison Shull, D. Botello

391 **BEAR'S DELIGHT** 5.5 **G**★

This is the prominent right-facing corner at the left end of the ledge above LICHEN OR LEAVE IT and HELTER SKELTER. The bolts and pin of LICHENING BOLT will be on the face to your right.

#1 Climb the corner to its top. Finish on GUNSIGHT TO NORTH PEAK or descend from cold shuts at the top of LICHENING BOLT (40 ft.).

FA John Christian, W. Putnam 1971

392 **LICHENING BOLT** 5.10b **R**

(Var.) Climb the face directly above the end of LICHEN OR LEAVE IT. Move past two bolts and a poor fixed pin to the anchor bolts.

FA Tom Cecil, Steve Cater 1988

Bring TCUs or the like to back up the pin. There is a 10–15 foot runout section on 5.7–5.8 rock at the top.

393 **SOME THINGS NEVER CHANGE** 5.10a **PG**

Find the bolted face behind and right of the tree at the top of the first pitch of ROUX.

#1 Climb straight up the textured face past several quarter-inch bolts. Move right to belay at the crusty old pin anchor above BLUE HIGHWAY, or move on up to the summit ridge.

FA Herb Laeger, Howard Doyle 1991

394 **BLUE HIGHWAY** 5.9 **PG**

#1 Climb the face above FINGER STINGER. Climb pockets past a bolt.

FA Mike Artz, Gene Kistler 1985

395 **TRAVELER'S REST** 5.11b **PG**

Begin 15 feet right of BLUE HIGHWAY.

#1 Climb past two bolts, then move left to easier ground.

FA Eddie Begoon, Howard Clark 1989

396 **SCREAMLINE** 5.10b **X**

Begin back down on the ground 10 feet to the right of ROUX. Start about 15 feet left of the clean, shallow FINGER STINGER corner. This route is directly below the rappel tree at the top of the first pitch of ROUX.

#1 Climb the face and cracks to the trees above (55 ft.).

FA Mel Banks, Greg Hand 1978

Most often top-roped.

397 **INNOCENCE** 5.12a **R/X**

Start on SCREAMLINE.

#1 Climb 6–8 feet of SCREAMLINE, to a bucket/horn, and step right to a right-slanting hairline crack. Follow this crack to a horizontal crack, then head straight up the unprotected face to join FINGER STINGER at its upper corner.

FA Ed Begoon 1989

Take a selection of brass and/or steel micronuts.

398 **FINGER STINGER** 5.8 **R/X**★

Start beneath a shallow, smooth, left-facing corner about 20 feet right of the ROUX corner.

#1 Climb the shallow corner to its top, just below the overhang. Move up and left until the flakes reach a narrow left-facing corner. Follow the corner to the large pine atop the first pitch of ROUX (65 ft.).

#2 Finish on ROUX.

FA Herb Laeger, Eve Uiga

Unfortunately, the initial narrow corner of this excellent line is an expanding flake. On at least two occasions apparently good pro pulled out, resulting in ground falls.

Connie Tseng tackling the crux of ROX SALT (5.7). (Photo: Bill Webster)

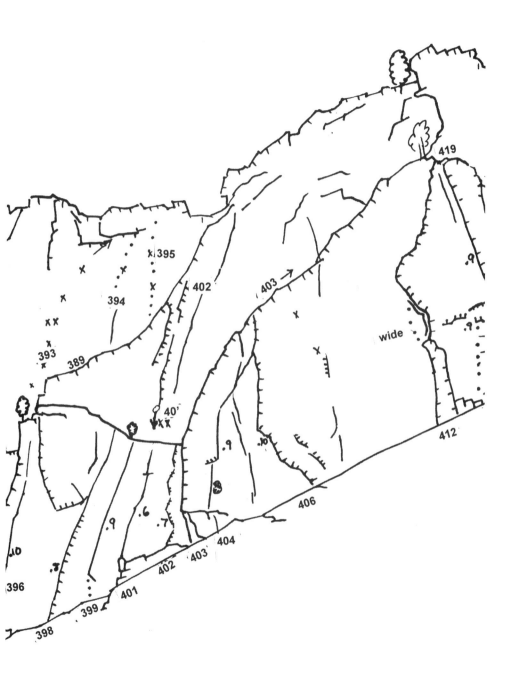

399 UNRELENTING VERTICALITY 5.9 PG★

This is the prominent crack that starts a short distance above the ground and diagonals up and right, just to the right of FINGER STINGER.

#1 Climb the crack to a small tree on a decent ledge. Use the tree as a directional and move right about 15 feet to a bolt anchor (75 ft.).

#2 Above is a crack that has a tree growing from it. Climb the crack, and end with an easy hand traverse to the left (100 ft.).

FA Herb Laeger, Eve Uiga, Charlie Rollins 1974

An excellent route, though the crux moves near the ground are difficult to protect.

400 CHALK PARTY 5.9 R/X

Begin about 10–15 feet right of UNRELENTING VERTICALITY and just left of the diagonal crack of ROX SALT.

#1 Climb the thin, left-facing corner to its top. Traverse right across the face to a ledge. Step up and climb a poorly protected face to intersect with the top of UNRELENTING VERTICALITY (60 ft.).

FA Eric Janoscrat, Mark Shissler 1982

401 ROX SALT 5.6 G★

About 25 feet right of UNRELENTING VERTICALITY is another right-leaning crack.

#1 Climb the crack up and right to face moves below the ledge. Stop at the bolt anchor that is also used by UNRELENTING (40 ft.).

FA Howard Doyle, Lotus Steele 1977

402 REALLY FLAKY 5.7 R

Start several feet to the right of ROX SALT, just past a small pine growing about 6 feet up.

#1 Climb a short, thin flake to the shallow, discontinuous, left-facing corner system. Awkward face moves and stemming lead to the same ledge and anchor as ROX SALT (35 ft.).

#2 Climb straight up to a small tree at an overhanging slab. Move left under the slab, then up, to finish on ROUX (60 ft.).

FA Steve Beck, Ed Lacroix 1978

If you could be sure the pitons were good, this pitch might not rate an R.

403 SALLY'S PERIL 5.5 PG

Begin 2 feet right of REALLY FLAKY.

#1 Climb the left-facing cracks and face to a small vegetated ledge. Climb a short left-facing corner and move right to a large tree ledge (50 ft.).

#2 Scramble along the ledge, then move up and right to the base of a prominent detached flake (80 ft.).

#3 Climb the chimney up to the summit (50 ft.).

FA Chuck Sproull, Sally Jordan, Peter Gardiner 1971

404 GREAT IMPOSTOR 5.9 PG★

Start between SALLY'S PERIL and the next left-facing corner system of PSYCHOPROPHYLAXIS. Begin below a crack that diagonals up and right.

#1 Climb the rough face and cracks up and right past to a small bush. Protect carefully and continue up and right along the more obvious crack, past a runout section to the ledge and large tree of SALLY'S PERIL (80 ft.).

#2 Move left across a ramp for 15 feet, to a left-facing corner. Climb the corner and face past an expanding, detached flake to reach the summit (45 ft.).

FA Marty McLaughlin, Howard Doyle, Jim Annex 1979

The second pitch is nothing to write home about.

405 WIRE BLISS 5.10d R

Start just left of the PSYCHOPROPHYLAXIS corner and right of GREAT IMPOSTER.

#1 Climb up toward the obvious crack system in the middle of the face. Climb the crack and the slight bulge at its end. Step left and finish on GREAT IMPOSTOR.

FA Howard Doyle, Eric Janoscrat

406 PSYCHOPROPHYLAXIS 5.10b PG★

Start below the first obvious left-facing inside corner to the right of SALLY'S PERIL.

#1 Climb just left of the corner using flakes and cracks. Meet and climb the corner to its top. Move up and right to the large tree on SALLY'S PERIL (75 ft.).

#2 From the tree, climb the face past an arching left-facing corner straight to the top (35 ft.).

FA Greg Hand, Hunt Prothro, Herb Laeger 1975

There is an unprotected stretch of 5.8 rock near the end of the first pitch.

407 SPRINGTIME 5.8 R

(Var.) From the end of the first pitch of PSYCHOPROPHYLAXIS go straight up the face past a small left-facing, arching corner.

FA Howard Doyle, Marty McLaughlin

408 SKIN BRACER 5.10 R/X

Begin about 8 feet right of the PSYCHOPROPHYLAXIS start, beneath an inside corner.

#1 Climb the corner to the roof. Pass over the roof and into a left-facing corner. Follow the corner to a stance. Step right and climb over a bulge. Move back left and up a blank face to the tree (80 ft.).

FA Chris Kulczycki, Chris Rowins 1978

There is some loose rock.

409 STATIC KLING 5.11a R

Begin about 15 feet right of the PSYCHOPROPHYLAXIS start, just right of the corner.

#1 Climb cracks and overlaps for 20 feet. Traverse right about 7 feet, to a right-facing corner/flake. Make two moves up to clip a bolt. Continue up and slightly left, then back right, to a bolt below a broken orange crack/groove 50 feet up. Finish on the crack.

FA Howard Doyle, Eric Janoscrat

Hooks are recommended to protect the territory between the bolts. Remember to place pro at the end of the traverse before moving to the first bolt.

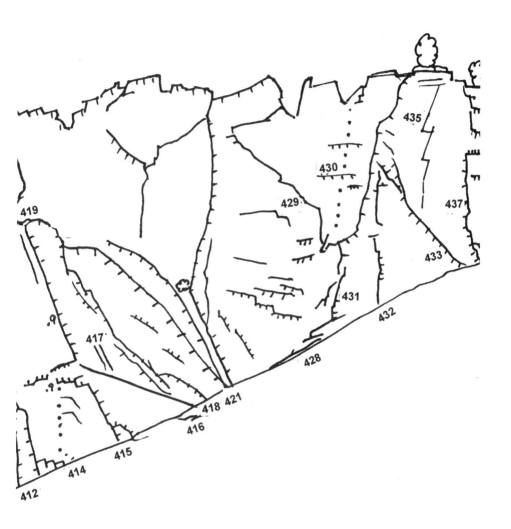

410 **THE MEMORIAL** 5.10a **X**

Start 10 feet right of STATIC KLING at an orange-and-black face.

#1 Move up the black streak and loose black flake. The runout occurs high on the pitch.

FA Pete Absolon

Dedicated to the memory of Buck Harper.

411 **PERMANENT PRESS** 5.9 **X**

Begin about 12 feet right of MEMORIAL and the same distance left of the start of WOLERY.

#1 Climb the wall past left-facing corners and flakes for about 30 feet. Move left and up toward a scooped-out area with orange rock. Step back right to a lichen-covered wall and climb straight to the top (100 ft.).

FA Howard Doyle, Lotus Steele

412 **WOLERY** 5.6 **PG**

Near the center of the North Peak–East Face there is a very prominent left-facing, right-trending corner system with a blocky pillar at its base.

#1 Climb to the top of the pillar. Move up and climb a groove up and left until it is possible to traverse back right to gain the corner. Follow the corner to the top of the flake (60 ft.).

#2 Step right and climb the corner to the summit (30 ft.).

FA John Christian, W. Putnam 1971

Bring a few 4- to 5-inch pieces.

413 **UNLIMITED SKY** 5.10c **R**

Begin several feet right of WOLERY, about 10–15 feet left of the next obvious left-facing corner of DESPERADO DIRECT.

#1 Climb through the overhang and continue up the face past a bolt.

FA Don Womack, John Govi 1985

414 **DESPERADO** 5.9 **PG★**

Start approximately 15 feet right of WOLERY and several feet left of the next obvious left-facing corner of DESPERADO DIRECT.

#1 Climb the face past thin cracks to a pointed horn at the left end of a small ledge. Cams work well here. Reach over and hand-traverse right, then pull up to a left-facing corner. Climb the 50-foot corner past another 5.9 move to a ledge (75 ft.).

#2 Finish on WOLERY.

FA Buddy Guthrie, Dee Dee Guthrie

415 **DESPERADO DIRECT** 5.11b **PG/R** ★

(Var.) From the ground, climb straight up the left-facing corner to reach the overhang.

FA John Bercaw, Dennis Udall

416 **BANDITO** 5.9 **G** ★

Begin 25 feet right of DESPERADO DIRECT.

#1 Rail out the clean diagonal crack up and left until it joins DESPERADO (50 ft.).

FA Hunt Prothro

417 **POWERS OF TEN** 5.10a **R**

Use the same start as BANDITO.

#1 Climb BANDITO out to the wide vertical slot. Climb straight up through the wide slot onto the face. Continue up the face to the top (75 ft.).

FA Paul Anikis, Mark Thesing, Pete Absolon

The protection is difficult. A custom-made piece was originally used for the wide slot.

418 **FAMAP** 5.8 **R**

Start a few feet right of BANDITO.

#1 Climb shallow, arching, right-facing flakes and corners to a tree.

 FA Eric Janoscrat, Barb Janoscrat 1983

419 **PROMISCUITY** 5.7 **PG**

Start beneath the tree at the end of the first pitch of CHRISTOPHER ROBIN.

#1 Follow corners directly to the tree (40 ft.).

420 **BURRITO MAN** 5.8+ **R/X**

Start just a few feet right of the FAMAP flakes, but left of the CHRISTOPHER ROBIN ledge start and the obvious EXPOTITION gully.

#1 Climb the short, indistinct left-facing corner to its top. Move left to flakes. Climb straight up to a ledge. Move left 10 feet, to a broken corner just right of a tree. Climb straight up to the CHRISTOPHER ROBIN traverse ledge (80 ft.).

FA Eric Janoscrat, Mike Artz 1984

The flakes are loose and the protection is poor.

421 **CHRISTOPHER ROBIN** 5.2

Start about 70 feet to the right of the very large left-facing WOLERY corner/flake, at the base of an obvious gully.

#1 Scramble up and left along a narrow ledge to a large pine tree (40 ft.).

#2 Continue left on the ledge, then climb a crack to bypass an overhang. Continue to the top (50 ft.).

FA U.S. Army 1944

422 **EXPOTITION** 5.2

Begin at the same start as CHRISTOPHER ROBIN, but go straight up.

#1 Climb the gully right of CHRISTOPHER ROBIN to the base of an inside corner facing left. Climb the corner (some loose rock), then step right about 5 feet to a crack. Climb the crack to an intersection with the second pitch of ROUX (100 ft.).

#2 Climb left of the notch.

FA Maitland Sharpe, Linda Harris 1971

423 **QUESTION MARK** 5.3

#1 At the top of the EXPOTITION gully, climb up and left toward a notch in the skyline (95 ft.).

FA Tom Stenger, Rick Varner

424 **BLUE EYES** 5.7
Use the same start as QUESTION MARK.
#1 Climb a slightly overhanging corner up and right for 35 feet. Continue up and right over small flakes to a ledge beneath the summit (90 ft.).
FA Bruce Cox, Judi Cox 1983

425 **LAZY DAZE** 5.7
#1 Climb the face on the right side of the EXPOTITION gully. Climb the crack and finish with an offwidth (90 ft.).
FA Rick Fairtrace, Linda Briskey, Bruce McCellan 1983

426 **OCTAVE DOCTOR** 5.9 **PG**
Begin just right of LAZY DAZE and the EXPOTITION gully.
#1 Climb shallow, left-facing corners/flakes until they end. Step left, around the outside corner. Continue to climb up the face and crack to a ledge. Climb easier rock to a good ledge with fixed pins (60 ft.).
#2 Climb straight past the pin on flakes and knobs to a ledge. Climb a short crack to the summit (40 ft.).
FA Sandy Fleming, Johnny Robinson 1982

427 **NACHO MAN** 5.10d **R/X**
Start 20 feet right of BURRITO MAN.
 #1 Climb the left-facing flake, then move right onto the face.
FA Mike Artz, Eric Janoscrat 1985

428 **LONG LEGGEDY BEASTIES** 5.4
Begin below and left of the prominent V-shaped notch on the skyline.
#1 Climb the face directly up to the ledge that lies 10 feet to the left of the V-shaped notch (40 ft.).
FA Maitland Sharpe, Linda Harris 1971

429 **POOH'S CORNER** 5.1

Begin below and just right of the prominent V-shaped notch.
#1 Climb easy left-angling ledges and an inside corner just to the right of
the notch. Walk right into the notch (60 ft.).
FA U.S. Army 1943

430 **OH POOH** 5.1

#1 Climb directly up from a point near the base of POOH CORNER to the
smaller notch to the right (60 ft.).
FA U.S. Army 1943

431 **HEFFALUMP TRAP DIRECT** 5.3

#1 Climb the left-facing corner/gully system with large flakes to the right
of the smaller notch in the skyline. This corner/gully system forms the left
side of the STREPTOCCOCUS wall.
FA U.S. Army 1943

432 **HERPES** 5.7+ **R/X**

Begin on the left side of the large orange STREPTOCOCCUS wall.
#1 Climb orange-colored flakes and shallow left-facing corners to a small
ledge. Continue up the short overhanging corner to the left and then up the
outside corner to the top, meeting HEFFALUMP TRAP DIRECT (45 ft.).
This climb has almost no protection but is easily top-roped.

433 **HEFFALUMP TRAP** 5.3 **PG**

Start 20 feet right of HERPES and about 50 feet left of the north end of the
cliff, at the center of the broad, orange STREPTOCCOCUS wall.
#1 Climb up and left along the flake formed by the long diagonal break
(40 ft.).
#2 Finish up the large left-facing corner.
FA U.S. Army 1943

434 FALSE LABOR 5.10c R/X

This route is squeezed between the start of HEFFALUMP TRAP and STREPTOCOCCUS.

#1 Climb the face just left of the striking finger cracks of STREPTOCOCCUS.

FA Don Womack, Herb Maher, Mike Gray 1985

435 STREPTOCOCCUS 5.9 G★

Start about 50 feet left of the north end of the cliff at the base of a thin crack system in the excellent orange wall. The HEFFALUMP TRAP diagonal break heads left from here.

#1 Climb the face up to a steep right-leaning crack in the orange rock. Follow the crack to its end at horizontal cracks. Move up and over the bulge to the top (50 ft.).

FA Howard Doyle, Lotus Steele 1977

436 SKOSHI GO JU 5.10c R/X

Start just right of STREPTOCOCCUS.

#1 Climb the broken face to a small ledge. Climb straight to the top.

FA Don Womack, Mike Cote

The protection is poor. The climb does not use holds on STREPTOCOCCUS or ISADORA'S RUN. This is a fairly squeezed route—a better TR var.

437 ISADORA'S RUN 5.4 PG★

Begin about 15 feet from the north end of the cliff.

#1 Climb the right-facing corner and pull the overhang. Continue to the top of the cliff (25 ft.).

FA Bill Webster, Isadora Duncan Brown 1976

SENECA TRAIL IV, 5.8

This is more than a girdle traverse; it's a circumnavigation of the entire Seneca Rocks formation. The route was established over a period of two years via rope solo. The final push was a 14-hour, 40-pitch, 3,000-foot effort.

P.1–2 Climb the first two pitches of ECSTASY (5.7).

P.3 Climb the SJM–ECSTASY CONNECTION to the black gully (5.6).

P.4 Cross the gully above the pine and mount the Totem Buttress on the Southwest Corner (5.1).

P.5 Cross the Totem Buttress on the obvious breakdown (5.1).

P.6 Traverse the finger lip/crack into TONY'S NIGHTMARE, then move down toward the tree. Look for a baby angle pin (SHAMBLER crux). Scramble up to the SKYLINE TRAVERSE belay tree (5.8).

P.7 Down-climb the second pitch of SKYLINE TRAVERSE (5.3).

P.8 Lead out on the east face on DUFTY'S, jump off on KAUFFMAN-CARDON, and belay at the obvious tree (5.5).

P.9 Follow KAUFFMAN-CARDON to Broadway Ledge (5.3).

P.10 Up A CHRISTIAN DELIGHT to OLD LADIES' (5.3).

P.11 Climb the second pitch of OLD LADIES' to its end (5.0).

P.12-13 Follow AMAZING GRACE to its end on Soler Flake (5.7).

P.14 Cross to CONN'S EAST to the end of the second pitch (5.5).

P.15 Two options: Finish CONN'S EAST, or from halfway up CONN'S EAST, traverse directly across the HIGH TEST area to above the Gryphon's Beak (5.8, the crux).

P.16 Down-climb GUNSIGHT TO SOUTH PEAK (5.3).

P.17 Cross northeast to the base of GUNSIGHT TO NORTH PEAK (5.0).

P.18 Down-climb obvious steps, turn north to the small pine halfway up LICHEN OR LEAVE IT (5.2).

P.19 Climb LICHEN OR LEAVE IT (5.8).

P.20 Traverse north to ROUX's first-pitch belay tree (5.0).

P.21 Traverse up and down and north to ROX SALT's first-pitch belay stance (5.2).

P.22 Traverse up and north to the large tree atop the SALLY'S PERIL flake pitch (5.3).

P.23 Follow easy ledge systems up, down, and north to the very base of HEFFALUMP TRAP (5.1). Don't touch down!

P.24 Climb HEFFALUMP TRAP. Stand on North Summit (5.3).

P.25 Very carefully scramble down to the top of No Dally Alley. Step cross, move south 20 feet, and down-climb the obvious ramp to the dark alley bottom (5.5).

P.26 Walk through No Dally Alley to the south entrance.

P.27 Climb WEST FACE TO GUNSIGHT until below the BELL.

P.28 Under the BELL, move down ledges until atop NOVA.

P.29 Move directly south to GREENWALL, pitch 2.

P.30 New pitch. Climb up and south across the white face to the PLEASANT OVERHANGS hanging belay (5.5).

P.31 Down-climb the second pitch of PLEASANT OVERHANGS (5.7).

P.32 Down-climb the second pitch of THAIS DIRECT (5.6).

P.33 Follow ledges west, then south, to WEST POLE.

P.34-35 Climb OLD MAN'S to the TRAFFIC JAM rappel tree.

P.36-37 Reverse HORRENDOUS TRAVERSE into Windy Notch (5.7).

P.38-39 Reverse the COCKSCOMB PINE TREE/OLD LADIES' traverse. From Luncheon Ledge, scramble south to the top of the Southern End, above ECSTASY JUNIOR.

P.40 Rappel to the ECSTASY JUNIOR/BURN wall area.

FA Mike Carroll, 1993/94

FA Continuous, Mike Carroll/Larry Singleton, 199

ERRATA

The following route information was gathered at a point in the production process that was too late to insert in the main body of the text. However, some of the routes are shown on photos.

North Peak—West Face
E1 Z MAN 5.13?
Start between SUMMERS EVE and NEGATIVE FEEDBACK.
#1 Climb past bolts to an anchor.
This is still at project status.

South Peak—West Face
E2 BEFORE THE FALL 5.10
Start near the base of THAIS.
#1 Stay right of THAIS and climb up somewhat crunchy, poorly-protected, but easy terrain past a bolt. Move right and belay at the THAIS ESCAPE ledge. (100 ft.)
#2 Climb straight up the wildly exposed fin to the top of the NUBILES flake. (90 ft.)
FA John Kelbel
The second pitch is stunning and well protected. For a better variation climb WEST POLE to the top of the second pitch. Climb down to the THAIS ESCAPE ramp and belay at the base of the fin, just left of NUBILES. Climb the spectacular fin to the top.

E3 DISCOUNT LION SAFARI 5.9+
This is a variation to the first pitch of THE BURN.
#1 Climb the first 40 feet of THE BURN to the ledge just before the bulge. Pull the bulge by going up and right until you are left of the arête and below a thin vertical crack system. Climb cracks to the ledge. (100 ft.)
FA Harrison Shull
Intricate gear placements are required.

E4 Z HOLE 5.7+

This is a variation to the seldom-done second pitch of THE BURN.

#1 Follow the crack up the face, but then wander out right until almost on the arête. Climb to the top of the South End. (100 ft.)

Don't expect to wait in line. The shaky pro and bad rock will likely keep the crowds down.

South Peak—East Face

The following 3 new routes are located on the Southeast Corner and are shown on the photo on pages 164 and 166.

E5 T & T 5.9

Start uphill from the start to SKYLINE TRAVERSE at the base of a smooth ramp.

#1 Climb to the top of the ramp and go up the face past several bolts and gear to the Kauffman Cardon Ledge and a two bolt anchor. (120 ft.)

#2 Climb up, trending left, past a small roof to Broadway Ledge. There may be a fixed anchor on a tree. (70 ft.)

FA Tom Cecil, Todd Offenbach 1990s

E5 R & R 5.6

Climb WORREL'S THICKET about thirty feet until you reach a small ledge on the left with 2 bolts.

#1 Climb up to the left-facing corner system and follow it to the end of KAUFMAN CARDON. (130 ft.)

FA Tom Cecil, Nick Sisk 1990s

E6 M & M 5.10

Scramble up WORRELL'S THICKET for about 100 feet to a point just right of a left-facing corner (R & R).

#1 Climb the thin face past small wire nut placements and 2 bolts to Lower Broadway Ledge.

FA Tom Cecil, Nick Sisk 1990s

INDEX

BY RATING